PRAISE FOR *PIVOT, DISRUPT, TRANSFORM*

"This book is an exceptional resource that will help leaders better understand how real leadership works; how to become comfortable with disruptive change; and how to create that change and thereby create your future. The alternative is to throw random solutions (i.e., best practices) at problems and hope for the best. If you're looking to open your mind to alternative understanding, this book is for you."

—DR. KENNETH M. MACUR,
President, Medaille College, New York

"This is a story about transformation and disruption, about recognizing and embracing change rather than ignoring and resisting it. This book fully recognizes the immense generational shift taking place with millennials and accepts that what influences and motivates them is significantly different than any generation that preceded them. Most important, the book provides actionable tools to help drive this change. This is an important read for anyone really interested in developing a highly functioning and modern business organization."

—DAVE ZUCHOWSKI,
President of Hyundai, 2007–2017

"*Pivot, Disrupt, Transform* is astonishing and leads you to a whole new world. You might hesitate to drop your old way of thinking that you learned at school or the way that you work. But this book deeply entices you to learn and turn around your thoughts and actions. You will see and experience the power of transformational change! Get on board and enjoy the ride!"

—KENJI FURUSHIRO,
President, Pasona N. A.

"Marcia Daszko's insights go beyond the obvious to root causes. Many problems in corporations and businesses could be alleviated by a true understanding of what Marcia has to offer in her latest book. W. Edwards Deming said it, and those who understood prospered. Marcia continues the work."

—PRISCILLA PETTY,
interviewer and producer, *The Deming of America*

PIVOT,
DISRUPT,
TRANSFORM

MARCIA DASZKO

PIVOT, DISRUPT, *TRANSFORM*

How Leaders Beat the Odds and Survive

DIVERSION
BOOKS

Diversion Books
A Division of Diversion Publishing Corp.
443 Park Avenue South, Suite 1004
New York, New York 10016
www.DiversionBooks.com

For more information, email info@diversionbooks.com

First Diversion Books edition October 2018.
Paperback ISBN: 978-1-63576-474-1
eBook ISBN: 978-1-63576-473-4

LSIDB/1810

DEDICATION

To my son and family:
Timothy, Terri, Owen, and Makoda Daszko
and Timothy's father, Gene Daszko

To my parents,
Mary Lou and James Sullivan

To my mentors in life and work:
Dr. W. Edwards Deming, Dr. Perry Gluckman,
Dr. Myron Tribus, Patsy Schmelzer, and Dr. Mark Shal

To my family, friends, and clients:
You are special in so many ways!

To all who inspired and encouraged me with love
and challenges, and who instilled in me a love of learning
and making a difference

To the natural leaders, heroes, entrepreneurs, and all
individuals with courage who make improvements, make a
difference, are transformative change catalysts, speak up, and
encourage others to ask questions and think different.
To all of you above, and those I haven't met yet, thank you!

▪ PREFACE ▪

Sometimes we can't predict what will happen in life. The change in my career path more than twenty years ago changed my thinking about my work, my life, and the way I raised my son. With new learning, I disrupted my thinking, pivoted the direction I was headed in life, and experienced a personal transformation. My life was great, but then it took on a new, bolder meaning.

My first ten-year career in corporate communications and marketing led me to work for Dr. Perry Gluckman and his team of management consultants and statisticians. His company, Process Plus, was known for helping corporations like HP, 3Com, and Dow Chemical learn and apply Dr. W. Edwards Deming's philosophy of leadership. After working there for a month, Perry asked me to do business development, and I asked, "What am I selling?" Perry sent me off to Dr. Deming's four-day seminar held at the historic Del Coronado Hotel in San Diego, California where more than 1,500 senior executives from diverse industries and other sectors such as education, healthcare, and the military listened to his messages. But Dr. Deming, age eighty-six then, was challenging to understand. For me, he used unfamiliar words like process (my experience had been in marketing semiconductor processes), control charts, systems thinking, etc.

After the four days, I went to Perry's office and said, "I don't know what he was talking about!" Perry said, "Don't worry, I'll teach you." The next three months I felt like I went through a PhD program. I read, studied, and had four- and five-hour long conversations every week or two with Perry. I also watched Perry give speeches and ask questions with our client executives, questions I had never heard before.

After a few months of intensive study and reading, I told Perry, "I want to hear Dr. Deming again." Off I went to my second four-day seminar. What a difference! His words began to make sense, and I began to connect the dots with his messages about leadership, quality, continual improvement, the fourteen points, variation, and systems thinking.

The conference organizer, Dr. Nancy Mann, introduced me to Dr. Deming. We quickly engaged in a deep discussion, though I told him that I was just beginning to learn. He invited me to dinner that evening with a small group of senior vice presidents, an admiral, and a colonel. I was excruciatingly shy then and hoped I wouldn't choke on my food. I listened and watched the interactions. After dinner, Dr. Deming told me to come to the four-day seminars as often as I could. I went every three months and attended twenty of his seminars in total. Dr. Deming became my mentor, too. And I was fortunate to also study and learn from other great systems thinkers such as Dr. Myron Tribus, Dr. Peter Senge, and Dr. Russell Ackoff.

Their guidance and philosophy about work and education changed my life. But in 1993, two of my key mentors (Dr. Gluckman and Dr. Deming) died. What would I do? Clients still needed our help, so I continued to work with them and founded Marcia Daszko & Associates in 1994. I made a choice to keep doing what I loved. I also felt an obligation to my mentors to make a difference. I love that the philosophy I have learned from so many great mentors and colleagues has the capacity to facilitate positive change among people who want to work, improve, and lead together.

One of the most important messages that Dr. Deming and Dr. Gluckman taught me was to continually learn and discover. I learned a lot about their principles by helping leaders apply them. My son reminded me when I was writing this book that my mentors taught me foundational theories and principles, but I created strategic questions and methods to help leaders apply and accelerate their transformation work. My learning continued with my family, friends, colleagues, and clients.

I base this book on what I have learned from my mentors, from working with my clients for more than twenty-five years on strategic leadership and transformation consulting, teaching MBA classes, and continually asking questions and observing how people lead, learn, interact, and celebrate together.

*Keep learning and discovering through applying these
and new principles.
Keep connecting the dots.*

CONTENTS

What *PIVOT, DISRUPT, TRANSFORM* Will Do for You

IT WILL PROVOKE YOU.

My aim is to provoke your current thinking, to challenge it, and to influence you to think and interact differently when you finish this book. A journey of personal transformation will not be easy, but it will be fulfilling and worth the time and energy.

IT WILL MAKE YOU UNCOMFORTABLE.

If you are uncomfortable with the ideas in this book, the message is getting through. My aim is not to make you comfortable, but to roust you out of your comfort zone and challenge you to adopt new, different, and more useful ways to lead, communicate, collaborate, and deliver meaningful value at home, work, and in society.

IT WILL INVITE YOU TO THINK LIKE NEVER BEFORE—AND THEN DO SOMETHING ABOUT IT.

The ideas I am presenting are not commonly practiced, but they have more common sense and theoretical foundation for quality improvement than those currently in use.

IT WILL MEASURE YOUR COURAGE, WHICH YOU WILL NEED TO IMPLEMENT ANYTHING NEW THAT YOU LEARN.

If you are an executive, manager, or person with a higher position or rank than others in your organization, you will need courage. This courage is personal. It demands that you examine your own beliefs, assumptions, and practices, and challenge them. Personal courage in reading this book means putting aside arrogance, greed, complacency, an autocratic management style, command-and-control behaviors, judgment of others, and possibly even narcissistic behaviors. It means doing the right thing for all rather than the right thing only for yourself. That may be quite a challenge for some, especially for those who think they are already doing the right thing, are entitled, and deserve to have the corner office with the big salary, bonus plan, and perks.

PIVOT,
DISRUPT,
TRANSFORM

A few years ago, at a nonprofit in the Midwestern U.S., there was an associate director who regarded herself as the Performance Appraisal Queen. She believed it was her duty and her right to judge, rank, and rate her employees. She took her task seriously and expected all of the other managers to do likewise. The employees and even the managers lived in a culture of fear, intimidation, and blame. At the first company off-site, I began teaching the management team. They experienced strategic thinking for transformation, rather than the traditional strategic planning session to which they had become so accustomed. It was during this off-site that the Performance Appraisal Queen threw away her crown entirely.

During a tense and interactive interchange, the associate director pompously argued that performance appraisals were good for employees, and it was her job to hold the individuals accountable. The managers watched the hour-long discussion, during which the associate director and I tenaciously plowed through the perceived pros, cons, and ramifications of performance appraisals. I listened to every argument the executive shared, calmly and firmly challenging each assumption as unfounded. Next, I suggested that we adjourn for the day and that the associate director look up the words "accountable" and "responsible" in the dictionary that evening. The associate director left the room convinced that the thinking and actions that she had practiced for so many years would prevail.

The next morning, there was a curious hush as people filtered into the room; they wondered how this session would begin—and how it would continue. After the normal morning greetings, the associate director spoke first, her eyes directed on me. She said in a different tone of voice from the previous day, "I am so sorry." "What are you sorry about?" I asked, truly puzzled. "I took so much of our time yesterday because I didn't understand the difference between responsibility and accountability. I no longer can be the Performance Appraisal Queen! And if I was so sure about this for so long, what else could I be wrong about?" Personal transformation was beginning to emerge.

The managers around the table were speechless. Less than twenty-four hours before, an executive leader was stuck in a belief and practice that was harming her people (who wanted to come to work every day and do a good job). In turn, she was harming their productivity, as well as the quality of the work her organization could produce.

I smiled and reassured her and the rest of the group, "This is the first step in a long journey of transformation. You will learn to challenge many of your beliefs and assumptions. You will examine and question if they really help you get closer to your aim in a healthy environment, or if they cause you to foster a dysfunctional environment and take you further away from your compelling purpose and your desired results." The team's energy for the rest of the day was contagious and just the beginning of the organization's turnaround.

Leaders have the job of creating a system that works for all. Whether they're leading a soccer team, family, Fortune 500 corporation, community, church choir, Army battalion, or nonprofit, leaders guide a system that either delivers results and achieves success and significance, or doesn't. Leaders create the system, and only they are accountable for optimizing the system.

Many leaders run their organization without thinking of it as a system and without thinking about the strategies and methods they use to improve it. They do not challenge themselves with enough questions to discover the opportunities for improvement. They settle for the status quo and what they've always done and known.

When we all learn, work, and improve together, we can transform the world. When we believe that survival is necessary (and it's not a given!) and we strive for sustainable prosperity, a system can become stronger. We must all play a part in creating a world—a system—that can work for everyone. It is the job of leaders to create and optimize the system (system optimization) they lead and to continually transform it. These two concepts are interrelated and interdependent. The work to apply them is essential for sustainable survival and growth.

Now is the time to increase our awareness and make decisions. How do we want to make a difference, lead and inspire people, grow healthy organizations, and survive? More than anything, it is time to challenge our thinking and the actions we take in our world. We can choose to go in new directions and anticipate and create what our future may hold. We can make bold, new decisions, and embrace the possibilities. Or we can keep things the way they've always been. Each time we arrive at a fork in the road, we will decide, "Should we go in the same direction, the direction we know and is in our comfort zone?" or, "Should we explore new possibilities, to stretch where we have never been before, where we cannot predict the outcomes, where we adapt, where we may embark on new but worthwhile struggles?" We are free to choose new answers.

WHY IS THERE FAILURE?

Some organizations are self-destructing and failing at a rapid pace. Twenty-three out of twenty-four businesses in the United States fail. More than 60 percent of the nation's largest corporations that appeared on the first Fortune 500 list in 1955 are not on the list today. Can you imagine Boeing, IBM, GE, Amazon, Ford, or Exxon disappearing? Yet Montgomery Ward, Lehman Brothers, DEC, Pan Am, Enron, and others have. There are still more than 2,000 companies that have been on the Fortune 500 list since 1955. Some will disappear, while other new innovators will disrupt the way we've done things in the past and emerge as global competitors.

We are dealing with climate change, budget deficits, crumbling school systems, increasing prison populations, a failing war on drugs, a growing gap between the wealthy and the poor, housing affordability issues, transportation challenges, an increase in mental illness and homelessness, shrinking productivity in American manufacturing, an aging infrastructure, more than 100,000 deaths a year in healthcare systems due to mistakes, and a global economy in disarray—to name a few! What is happening? What kind of thinking and interactions are creating these global and societal outcomes?

Organizations fail because their leaders maintain a mentality that the status quo is fine; their business or industry is not in danger of extinction. Most leaders are not aware that they need systems knowledge and an understanding of a theoretical framework that could help them develop and transform relationships and their organization in healthy and sustainable ways. The majority of today's leaders circulate internal, unsubstantiated beliefs, wrong assumptions and policies, and "best practices" and programs that, when implemented, create fear, internal competition, dysfunctional behaviors, poor productivity, and toxic cultures.

This book systematically identifies and challenges the thinking that creates the widely held and commonly implemented "best practices" that must stop and new ways that must start.

The purpose of this book is to help leaders (including natural leaders, not only formal leaders with positions and titles) discover their internal courage and support them to effectively perform the role of leadership: to personally transform and then to optimize their system. It offers those who want to succeed a choice: to transform, optimize, and succeed; or, to adopt beliefs and "best practices" that lead to struggle and failure. The choice seems easy. But transformation is not easy. Leadership takes guts!

Our world needs transformation and optimization because it has multiple challenges: wars, declines, attacks, riots, famine, corruption, fraud, arrogance and greed, elitism, obsession with money and consumerism, corporate ethics, measure mania, fear-driving reactive behaviors, ruthless and controlling power, judgments and blame, trade wars, climate change, and Wall Street's quarterly and short-term thinking. There are enough examples of the need for significant change that prompt the need for examining transformation.

A few years ago, management professor and author Margaret Wheatley opened a presentation with the words: "We live in a world of ruthless aggression. The time for sitting quietly is over; we can no longer be complacent." The audience took a deep breath, and there was a pregnant hush. What must we do? Pivot, disrupt (current thinking and behaviors), and transform.

It is possible for capable leaders to optimize and transform our systems. Systems can survive and grow. Or they can fail. What is the difference? Why do some leaders and organizations fail while others survive and flourish?

If leaders exhibit only tactical and analytical behavior without strategic, visionary thinking, systems will fail. This path toward failure is not necessary, yet it is the path that some leaders and organizations unknowingly choose. The survival of many systems depends on their leaders having systems knowledge and the courage to move beyond the accepted norms.

We must ask our leaders:

Why transform? What if we do not transform?

What if we are successful today? Is that enough?

Are we happy today with the results we see around the
world?

Survival is optional. How will leaders disrupt and pivot their thinking so they are able to transform their organizations and survive? Leaders should ask questions at every fork in the road: "Will we choose to make incremental improvements for mere change, or to transform into an organization that's bold, new, and different?" "Will we shift our interactions to work *together* to connect the dots, to communicate with each other toward a common aim, and to engage more fully to build relationships with sustainable goals in mind?"

If people are uncomfortable with change and intimidated by innovation, they will revert to traditional practices. But when people transform their thinking, it becomes impossible for them to go back to their old ways.

Pivot, Disrupt, Transform is for all of us who want to transform from caterpillars to butterflies. Join me on this journey to help you live life to the fullest potential, to continually learn and transform, and to lead and grow in ways you never imagined possible.

What Is Your Current Thinking and What Are Your Actions?

To begin, assess your own thinking.

Do you believe it is important to hold individuals accountable?

YES   NO

Do you believe it is critical to motivate your employees?

YES   NO

Do you make most of your decisions based on conversations and intuition?

YES   NO

Do you set targets and numerical goals for individuals to achieve?

YES   NO

Does the executive team have annual strategic planning meetings to create the vision, mission, strategies, numerical goals, objectives, and deliverables?

YES   NO

Does leadership create a lengthy mission paragraph for the company?

YES   NO

Does the organization continually adopt "best practices" and benchmark with other companies?

YES   NO

Is change management adopted in your company but not much changes? Is resistance to change common in your culture?

YES   NO

Do you believe the company should hire the best recruits with the best GPAs from the best schools to achieve the best results?

YES   NO

Does management focus on quotas, results, the bottom line, and the stock price?

YES   NO

Are reorganizations and restructuring common and frequent?

YES   NO

When times are difficult, do you quickly respond by cutting costs?

YES   NO

Do you believe you should empower employees?

YES   NO

Do you believe it is important to conduct annual performance appraisals and rank and rate the employees?

YES   NO

Do you score those appraisals and tie them to compensation and bonuses?

YES   NO

Do you incentivize workers with rewards and have a quota system?

YES   NO

Score:

If you answered yes to more than two questions, you need this book.

When you finish it, will you become the global leader we need?

What Leaders Must STOP Doing and Why

De-Motivate
Bullying Intimidate
Appraisals
Accountability Criticize STOP Slogans
Maximize Cut Judge Costs
Layoffs Fear Merit
Erode Win-Lose Reduce
Fads Blame Lose
Micro-manage
Competition
Arrogance
Incentives

This graphic illustrates an organization's traits and practices. Do these practices work together to create a healthy culture? Would this enterprise "wow" and serve customers? Would you experience joy in working here?

▪ INTRODUCTION ▪

Part One describes practices that must STOP. The "best practices" and management fads often lead to internal struggles, dysfunctional working environments, high turnover, low morale, and the imminent demise of the organization. Do you experience any of the following STOP practices where you work?

FOCUSING ON THE NUMBERS, METRICS, AND THE BOTTOM LINE

QUESTIONS FOR YOU
- How much time do you spend in meetings forecasting, budgeting, setting numerical targets, and reviewing the bottom line? Do you do it again and again, week over week, month over month, year over year?
- Does it help you achieve better results?
- Does anyone care about profit? Do you discuss the processes that can help create profit vs. loss?

The United States is known for its short-term focus. We want results and profits and the exit strategy executed—and we want it now! Whether it's meeting sales quotas, a certain profit number, or test scores on standardized tests, numbers are driving our behaviors. Oftentimes, the behaviors that emerge from trying to attain these number-driven results are dysfunctional, ugly, and toxic for long-term success. In this type of competitive environment, people learn to manipulate the numbers, the work, or their interactions with each other in order to meet a target number. People work around the system to satisfy a personal goal (to attain a promotion, a new title, or a raise). The tampering for personal gain begins, while the organization goes awry.

How can one make effective decisions when people are compromising or tampering with the numbers? What happens when the work processes are constantly being changed, resulting in more variation in the system? There is far too much focus on metrics, measures, big data, and analytics. (Some focus on the numbers and statistical analysis makes sense. But measuring everything without being able to connect how the statistical analysis leads to better decision making and achieving the strategic aim and the goals isn't helpful.) Effective leaders will need to step beyond the "big data" fad and instead make informed decisions, based on data in context, that aligns with the direction of the organization. For decades, executives have led their organizations based on a deep understanding of the company culture without succumbing to spread sheets and regression lines to dictate their judgment.

If leaders want different and better results, their focus must be on *improving the system and the processes within the enterprise that create those results,* rather than having a myopic view on the outputs themselves. Step one: improve or transform the system. Step two: review what the system delivers. To tamper with the numbers only means making adjustments after the fact.

EXAMPLE

On a hot, sunny morning, I looked out the window over the rolling hills of Santa Clara County and then turned back to my clients and challenged them to stop looking at the bottom line. No more poring for hours daily over the line items, no more looking at the weekly profit and loss statements, no more reacting to the stock price or labor costs, no more knee-jerk reactions to start-and-stop spending, no more short-term thinking about the numbers.

A few of the executives turned white, and a few others wondered how they were going to spend their time at work now. They swallowed hard as one squeaked out a quiet, "What?" I confidently announced, "We have a lot of hard work to do, work you have never done before, and we don't have the time to waste by looking at line items on budget sheets and moving around numbers. You're bleeding ink, and we need to shift your thinking before that ink becomes fluorescent. The only way to change your results is to change how you think and what you do. Together you, the leaders, will create a new system that engages all of the employees, focuses on creating an awesome customer experience, and allows everyone in the company to work *together* to improve and innovate. Only that radically new focus will shift the bottom line from a negative to a positive. You will disrupt your current beliefs, pivot in a new direction, and transform."

The executives had their challenges laid out in front of them: keep doing what they had been doing and deal with too much complexity, too many issues and problems, only to get the same unacceptable, recurring results—less than desirable. Alternatively, they could take a leap of faith, learn and implement a new approach, and potentially succeed—or even succeed like never before! But would they have the courage to step out of their comfort zone? They were committed to the stress, the waste and inefficiency (much of what they were blind to), and the overwhelming lists of initiatives to drive and problems to solve—it was familiar. Would the unknown be a better alternative?

The team diligently went to work. They adopted new systems thinking (focusing on how all of the parts would work together to achieve their purpose), focused on learning *together*, and began creating their new systems and processes, fostering a collaborative culture of *transformative* change (not merely tinkering around the edges and promoting "change for change's sake") and improvement *and* innovation systems. In a few months, they transformed the company from having a loss of $300,000 to having a $1.4 million profit in an extremely competitive industry.

Four months later, after many improvements in the systems,

processes, and environment, I said, finally, "Let's look at the numbers." The executive team looked at me with the same expressions of horror that they had on the day I had challenged them to stop poring over and manipulating the numbers. They couldn't believe I cared about the bottom line. I do care about the bottom line. But these leaders needed to learn to care about *more than* the bottom line. When the leaders and the entire organization cares about how all parts of the system interact (the purpose, the customers, the vendors, the staff, learning, data in context, resources, etc.), a healthier bottom line becomes the natural outcome.

Any responsible executive team cares about profits, but to achieve the profits, the leaders need to focus on their most important job: to lead people, transform the organization, and optimize a system (their organization with all of the interdependent parts working together) that will deliver great results. Focus on improving the system that delivers the outcomes, not the outcomes themselves.

As Dr. Myron Tribus admonished, "Looking at the results is like driving the car by looking in the rearview mirror." It's easy to tell where you've been. It's easy to see what your competitors are doing around you (that you may want to copy or benchmark). But it takes a leadership team having meaningful conversations, asking great and tough questions, and being aware and perceptive enough to identify a new future that makes the real difference.

LESSON

STOP focusing on the bottom line. Focus on improving or innovating the system that creates the results. If the results need to be different, focus on changing the system. Caring about and understanding the relevance of the bottom line is far different than obsessing over the bottom line. When the obsession is the bottom line, the company will not survive. When executives are focusing on the numbers and reacting to and tampering with them, they are not doing their job. Their job is to create an optimal system and environment for people to do great work and to serve customers and new markets. Leaders understand that the systems and processes deliver the results, some measureable and some immeasurable, some tangible and some intangible. If the results are not desirable, the results will only change when leaders change the system. Blaming and judging people (holding individuals accountable when they have no control of the system), or tampering with the numbers, won't improve the results.

SETTING INDIVIDUAL GOALS AND HOLDING INDIVIDUALS ACCOUNTABLE

QUESTIONS FOR YOU:

- Are you setting numerical goals and targets and expecting individuals to meet them?
- If the results you expect are not achieved, do you track down the person to blame?
- Do you have a clear purpose about what you want your team to accomplish? Can they do it?

Leaders, without intending to and while trying to do their best, often make a large but common mistake in their organizations. Besides having an obsessive focus on the bottom line, they are also consumed by managing a system that is full of setting individual goals and then holding individuals accountable for the results. What's wrong with this common practice? When the numbers aren't achieved, an environment of finger pointing, blame, and criticism emerges. Yet, it is the leaders who are ultimately accountable for the system outcomes. The leaders created the system.

Individualized goal setting and holding individuals accountable is a management fad, practiced by those who do not understand systems and how systems work. It's up to leadership to create a system so people can work *together* to achieve the goals they need in order to best serve customers. Individuals are *part of* the system that management has created. Individuals (employees) cannot change the system, therefore, they are not responsible for it. The only people who can change the system are the executives. Employees work IN the system. Management works ON the system to create a system that can be optimized for all.

Are you getting the results you want? If you're not, look to the system and not to the people. This is where great leaders excel. They understand that they are accountable for managing the system. Those who understand this essential and fundamental concept (systems thinking) are much more likely to achieve a competitive edge and higher quality for their constituents. Leaders must understand that when they don't get the results they want, it is the system that they created and set up that is not performing.

The people are just one part of the system. An individual is just one of many people, and people are one part of the larger system that also includes resources, knowledge, data, physical spaces, interactions, machines, training, marketing and sales, etc.! Barriers can be identified in any number of these parts of an organization. With a bird's eye perspective, the leaders must be able to look at the whole system and have the conversations to make a difference. All of the systems' parts need to work well *together*. If they don't, how and why does management pick out one part (the people) or one person to hold accountable?

The job of management is to study, improve, and/or transform the system. Leaders can ask themselves, what needs to be different about the system? Do people need resources or training or better direction or more effective communication with the customers? Do the materials or machines necessary for the job need to be upgraded? More than 90 percent of the issues and challenges faced in organizations are not caused by people. They are caused by poor systems. Bottom line: leaders own the system, and they are accountable for it.

Many managers think and feel they have every right to hold people accountable when the results aren't what they expect.

They react by moving people around (another reorganization!), blaming, demoting, judging, or even firing people. And they feel entitled to do this because that is how they think leaders lead. It is not.

Many managers have never been taught how to lead and develop people and manage systems, processes, plans, and budgets. And leadership and management are two different things (we'll delve into the difference in Part Three). Do managers ever stand back, reflect, and wonder, *what if I'm wrong?* If the struggles, frustrations, and poor results continue, the part of the equation that needs to change is staring at you in the mirror. That's quite a jolt to some executives and managers. But that jolt can also be the first transition step into being a leader, the awareness that a leader first develops and uses to inspire other people.

Many executives with positions and titles (referred to as formal or positional leaders) won't hold themselves accountable for the system they create and manage. They don't commit to new learning in a better way, especially if they are comfortable with or tolerant of the status quo or what they know. The daily struggles and challenges become an accepted part of doing business. The poor system becomes their reality. No need to rock the boat. They would rather deal with what they know, as frustrating as it might be, instead of going forward into the unknown, and being forced to change and improve.

To reiterate, what is a poor system? What causes it? We've earlier defined a system as a network of interdependent parts that has to have an aim/purpose. The key idea is that the system has to be led, not micromanaged. A system has to have a compelling purpose, clear communication to all staff about that purpose and how they can contribute to it, and many parts (and people) working together to accomplish the purpose.

The way management leads today (and has led for many decades), by pointing fingers and not evaluating the system as their own responsibility, is a common flaw. Understanding and leading a system correctly means leading the interactions and the interdependent parts to work together. When individuals, teams, or divisions are held accountable, leadership is doing parts thinking and not thinking about how the parts interact. A successful organization must embody holistic thinking and collaborate continually. Silo thinking refers to departments, individuals, or divisions (often called profit centers) within an organization that have their own set of goals, objectives, deliverables, and metrics that are independent from the rest of the organization. Resources, information, communication, or work does not flow. There is often internal competition between the parts instead of cooperation and collaboration. The linear thinking that supports working in silos, departments, and profit centers needs to stop.

Instead, leaders must create the opportunities for cross-functional teams and endorse working across the organization. Working in this capacity breaks down the barriers between people and departments and leads to a culture of creativity as people learn, support each other, and work toward their common strategic goals.

If leaders were able to fix the single flaw of holding individuals accountable, they would have a powerful impact on the productivity and performance in many organizations. Unfortunately, too many managers are not open to learning a new way to think and manage in a style that makes them feel like they know what they're doing. They will tolerate the struggles and frustrations of what they know rather than questioning and opening their minds to learning something they don't.

*It's wise to consider that there may be better ways to
lead and manage.*

The job of management cannot be delegated! Management is accountable for creating the system that people work in. Additionally, management must create the working environment where people are *self-motivated*. That's where the power of the people is. Leaders develop all of the natural leaders around them, and they must understand the specific role they fulfill and contribute to the whole.

People can engage, commit, and take responsibility for contributing their *part* to the success of the organization, but they can only do so when they have the right leadership, culture, training, and tools to do their jobs. If employees are in a poor system that has been developed by managers without systems knowledge, there is no hope that an individual can succeed without manipulating and distorting the numbers and the system for his own benefit. The system then produces a few winners, many losers, suboptimal results, and poor morale.

Next, executives without systems knowledge create performance management models, establish performance appraisals, and execute ranking and rating processes to hold individuals accountable. How much time do these "best practices" and management fads that create internal competition and toxic work environments waste? Have you calculated that wasted time? What if that time was used to develop, educate, and enhance skills, or to work *together* on improvement projects, new innovation ideas, or engage more and anticipate and understand customers' needs?

How many people love to be ranked and rated against the very colleagues with whom they are encouraged to collaborate and fulfill a compelling mission? Why doesn't it work? Mature adults do not want to come to work every week and put in fifty, sixty, or seventy hours of their best professional efforts to be judged, criticized, blamed, ranked, and rated. Instead, they want to do challenging, meaningful, fulfilling work that makes a difference. Managers who have to implement sub-optimizing processes (those processes that do not flow or work together because there are breakdowns in the processes that are outside of their control) get frustrated, stressed, and resentful about having to act like babysitters. Oftentimes they even have to spend their own free time analyzing each direct report and completing performance appraisals on their weekends at home. Hardworking, well-meaning employees get demoralized and eventually leave, either mentally or physically.

EXAMPLE

Let's assume that the Secretary of Education does not like the results the education system is producing—declining test scores, more dropouts, etc. He/she says, "We'll hold the state education departments accountable." Results are still poor. The states respond with, "We'll hold the school superintendents accountable." Still poor results! The superintendents say, "We'll hold the principals accountable." Results continue to tank! Principals explain, "We must hold the teachers accountable." The teachers, with all of their mighty resources, exclaim, "We must hold the kindergartners accountable!" Finally! The buck stops here!

Does it make sense? How is this system powerful? Should we hold a five-year-old accountable for the U.S. school system? This kind of thinking runs rampant across the United States and makes as much sense in business, healthcare, or the military as it does in education. Leaders are passing the buck instead of working to transform and optimize the system, which is a core function of their responsibilities. But do leaders understand what their job is? Or are they floating along with the fads that caused more than 60 percent of the Fortune 500 corporations to fail in the past seventy years? Will 90 percent of the startup companies in Silicon Valley continue their rate of failure? Ninety percent of the merger and acquisition transactions flounder and fail. What is missing from the integration process that leads to such a high failure rate? A new philosophy of leadership and a strategy to apply it is needed and available for those who want to learn and lead differently.

LESSON 1

STOP creating individual goals and holding individuals accountable for the performance of the system. The leaders who create the system are those who are accountable for it. When individuals are held accountable, thousands or millions of dollars are thrown away annually in wasted time spent on performance appraisals, performance management models, performance improvement plans (PIPs), and more recruiting and onboarding hours due to higher turnover, etc. These practices generate stress and low productivity due to employees' waning enthusiasm and disengagement. Continually recruiting new employees after the demotivated workers leave is an excessively high expense for organizations. There are several websites such as Glassdoor, Indeed, Vault, and CareerBliss that provide jobseekers with employee reviews of their companies and CEOs. They're good resources for people who want to research where to make their next career move and gain insight around executives who are leading their employees, optimizing a system that works for all, and creating a healthy culture.

Use these reviews as a learning opportunity. For example, of the more than 3.7 thousand employee reviews on Salesforce's Glassdoor company page, many of the resounding themes are: "visionary CEO," "collaborative colleagues," and "above and beyond in company culture." However, the reviews also reflect consistently on Salesforce's competitiveness and hard metrics to maintain. Overall, according to Glassdoor, 98 percent of its employees approve of the CEO, and 87 percent would recommend working there. This illustrates that even though the employees work in a challenging and competitive workplace, they are still advocates for Salesforce because of the leadership.

Leaders build an organization (system) that produces the outcomes that are needed now and for the future. They strive to create a system that can adapt to change and continually improve until it delivers the desired results. They engage the employees in helping make a system that is effective, adds value, makes sense, and serves customers. As illustrated by Salesforce, when the leaders create a system where the employees feel they can contribute, they flourish.

LESSON 2

Being accountable and being responsible are two different concepts, and each must be applied differently. Leadership is held *accountable* for the system that it created and for the system's results. The people are *responsible* for contributing their part to help the system deliver its outcomes.

Employees have a responsibility to contribute to help achieve the goals of an organization. But it is only the leaders who can be held accountable for the results, outcomes, and stock price. The leaders design the system that create the results.

USING PERFORMANCE APPRAISALS, 360 FEEDBACK, AND GRADES

QUESTIONS FOR YOU:

- Do you feel that you are helping people when you give them an appraisal that ranks and rates them?
- How many hours do you, or other employees and managers in your organization, spend judging a person, documenting, and communicating performance appraisal activities? What does that equate to in dollars?

We begin to prepare for giving or receiving performance appraisals when we are in grade school. Being judged for our performance and what we get wrong and right begins with gold stars, rewards, and grades. We're conditioned at an early age to work individually and have our work judged. We receive various forms of feedback, some of it helpful, some so harsh and critical that it devastates us, whether we are young or old.

Let's examine some of the common practices that are used for children and adults and often yield similar results. Which have you experienced?

TIMMY AND THE LOVE OF LEARNING

When my son was ready to go to kindergarten, I thought that he would experience the same kind of school system I had. Sometimes I was intimidated by some of my teachers and, undoubtedly, the principal. We had grades, gold stars, different levels of reading groups, and we were often given exercises to compete against each other. Over time, and with hours of homework, learning was sometimes an exasperating drudgery, even though I was an honor student. But I saw other students struggle. They didn't have the support system or encouragement that I had at home, nor did they have an innate love of reading. Over time I saw those students disengage and lose their joy in learning.

Fortunately, as a young mom sending my son off to school, I was introduced to some new concepts by some of my mentors, colleagues, and authors (Dr. W. Edwards Deming, Dr. Perry Gluckman, Alfie Kohn, Tom Coens, and Mary Jenkins), who suggested removing evaluations such as grades, gold stars, rankings, and ratings—all devised to pit person against person and create internal competition rather than an atmosphere of cooperation. What if we didn't make learning a contest?

Sports are games, and we can compete. But our education is important. We need people learning and working *together* to discover the cure for cancer or to invent the next transportation vehicle or to discover an effective way to clean up our oceans. What if there was joy in learning, not just in first grade but in sixth, ninth, and twelfth grades? What if we didn't have gold stars, internal competition (except for sports), grades, and honor rolls? What if we could all experience joy in learning and helping each other and excelling at subjects that we loved? Might a radical approach also impact the epidemic of bullying and harassment in schools and at work?

Many system thinkers taught me that the joy of lifelong learning was one key to happiness. Because of their philosophies, I changed how I raised my son. We didn't focus on grades, gold stars, rewards, or awards in our house. Instead, I asked my son two questions after school: "Did you have fun? What did you learn?" The two were interrelated. He grew up with a love of learning instilled, and I watched his teachers to be sure that his creativity and thirst for knowledge were not stifled.

In first grade, letter grades were introduced at his school and used on the children's papers and report cards. The second week of school, the faculty held a Parents' Night so parents could meet their children's new teachers and learn their classroom philosophies and plans for the school year. After my son's teacher shared her ideas, she asked us if we had any questions. My question to this nervous but sweet first-year teacher was, "Why do you grade?" The look on her face told us that she had never been asked or even considered this question before. Her thinking might have been, "I am a teacher; therefore, I grade."

I understood that. Years ago, I had been a seventh-grade teacher. I know firsthand that grading is what teachers do. It's what they've always done. It's what most students have experienced for decades. Why would we question grades? But why wouldn't we question grades? What about questioning anything that might hinder our children's learning?

After a short discussion about the impact of grades and how the research shows that, by the third grade in school, grades negatively impact the creativity of children and demotivate them, we made a new decision. The parents, the new teacher, and I decided to abandon grades. We started in my son's class, and, by the time he went through Grades 1-6, the whole school adopted the thinking. We didn't want our children graded. We wanted our children's teacher to instill a love of learning, to tap into her passion for why she went into teaching, and to create a classroom full of curiosity and the joy of learning. The focus would be on learning and understanding what the children understood and where they needed help. It wasn't about getting it wrong, making mistakes, and getting a "D." Every child would learn in different ways and at different times.

Maybe not grading would be a risky experiment that would

fail. Maybe! But if we didn't test some new ideas, we'd never learn if there might be a better way to engage students and instill a love of lifelong learning and curiosity.

My son and his classmates didn't receive grades until after they changed schools in the seventh grade. By the time he entered the real world of grades, he had already developed a deep love of learning, and no one could take that value away from him. He went on to triple major at the University of California Santa Cruz, graduating in four years while working part-time. After graduation, he decided to get an Emergency Medical Technician (EMT) certificate. Then he applied to and was ultimately chosen to enter the San Jose Police Academy, a one-year intensive program. Now he's a fraud investigator, and the learning continues.

Grades are a precursor for what has evolved in the work place: performance appraisals. Would grades prepare us for getting judged, ranked, and rated in the workplace? How are those working for us?

Hundreds of research studies, articles, and speeches have been presented that suggest that the almost one-hundred-year-old practice of giving performance appraisals can be improved. Hundreds of other studies in the past ten to twenty years show the toxic impact that performance appraisals have on people, productivity, morale, collaboration, and teamwork, and organizations' results, bottom line, and yes, **profits.**

THE QUESTIONS MOST LEADERS HAVE NEVER ASKED

It's essential for courageous leaders to ask the bold, imperative questions about performance appraisals! What's our purpose and aim in using appraisals? What are our strategies? Are they effective? What are the outcomes? Do they help us get closer to our vision or further away? Do they help create collaboration and teamwork or internal competition? How long does it take for our managers and staff to implement this process? What are the results and outcomes? Do they help us have a robust, dynamic learning environment? Do they help us coach, mentor, and develop our people? Or do they instill fear and resentment?

Does management use performance appraisals to judge, blame, and rate individuals on their performance when instead, they need to be focused on how the system performs? What are the results of the system?

Many organizations across the U.S. have never asked these questions. They have adopted a process of judging, ranking, and rating their employees. The practice is mired in incorrect assumptions about the necessity of appraisals. Human resource and talent management departments justify this practice by assuming appraisals must be given for the organization to understand who needs to be:

- laid off if the company needs to cut costs
- terminated with documentation
- coached
- promoted
- aligned with the performance management tool (another fad?)

Tom Coens and Mary Jenkins wrote a seminal book that every leader needs to explore. Based on four years of research, Tom, a labor attorney, and Mary, an HR senior executive at General Motors, challenged and debunked all of the assumptions I list above. In their book, *Abolishing Performance Appraisals*, they write, "Each organization has two choices in dealing with the futile process of appraisal. Choice one is to appease everyone by continuing the practice, promoting the illusion that appraisal works and pretending not to notice the harmful side effects. Choice two is to begin an organization-wide initiative of education in which you help people understand why appraisal fails and then, together, work on strategies to replace appraisal, looking for genuinely new ways to actually deliver on the high hopes that were placed in appraisal."[1]

There are two significant umbrella issues that illustrate the devastating impact of using performance appraisals. First, most performance appraisals **destroy** people. When people feel judged, criticized, and blamed, they are not mentally engaged, motivated, happy, or healthy. Second, performance appraisals **destroy** the health and impair the success of organizations. When people are devastated, unappreciated, undervalued, or unrecognized for their contributions, productivity decreases while absenteeism and turnover increase.

How many people love to **get** performance appraisals? Except for the few people who continually get great scores, the majority of employees are demotivated after receiving their appraisal. They resent the process and sometimes even the messenger. They disengage from the work they may have been happy with and withdraw their contributions and efforts. Even if they did well on the appraisal, they are often demoralized because they do not agree with some of the comments or their ranking or rating. Few things can build resentment faster than a performance appraisal gone awry—and most do go awry. Some people speak up; others speak with their actions. They withdraw and are no longer the vibrant contributors they once were until they find a new position and resign. Some are emotionally devastated and never recover.

How many people love to **give** performance appraisals? Most managers procrastinate getting their performance appraisals done and turned into HR. It's often not a pleasant conversation between the manager and employee, especially when a manager feels like a judge of another person. Managers often feel compelled to point out flaws and criticize people. Even if they think that's their job, it doesn't feel good for either party. Additionally, this process is time consuming and takes everyone away from their real work. Managers and employees are anxious. Even when the conversation is pleasant, one hurtful comment is often exacerbated. A hardworking "star" employee can be traumatized when the manager's appraisal doesn't reflect the commitment the "star" has had.

What is the cost of the performance appraisal process to an organization? Depending on the size of their department, managers can spend an average of two hundred hours per year completing, conducting, and reviewing appraisals for their employees. At the minimum, let's say that an organization with one hundred managers has an appraisal process that costs $20,000 in time (managers, employees, and HR documentation). Can you imagine the cost for organizations like the military, government agencies, universities, or public corporations with more than fifty thousand employees? It's millions of dollars of waste! What can replace the waste? Leadership!

A LEADER RESIGNS

Years ago, Harry Artinian was Manager of the Americas at General Electric. CEO Jack Welch was kicking off his new Six Sigma program (a set of tools used for process improvement with the goal to achieve a six sigma statistical measurement), and Harry was chosen to lead a team of twelve GE "star" employees. These high-potential employees were from all parts of the corporation, also called "high pots" and GEMS (for GE Medical System). Their role was to produce the highest quality medical equipment. Each one of them was brilliant, as was their work together. After a year, GE's corporate HR told Harry that he had to give them performance appraisals and rank and rate all of the stars; some would get As while others might get Bs or Cs. Harry asked, "What? Did they get stupid in the last year? You can't take twelve people who are stars and, in a year, tell them they're not as good." He resisted, but HR won, and he reluctantly administered the appraisals, giving two of them Bs and the rest As. He and his team made it through the process that year relatively unscathed. The next year, HR again demanded the same process be followed. But Harry knew the outcome of ranking and rating people. He had seen it in previous companies: in time it would destroy teamwork and the high-quality results they were achieving together. Harry decided he was not going to take another chance of demoralizing, demotivating, or hurting his people who were fully committed to doing great work together. So he resigned, moving to another corporation where he could inspire and develop his team to work together.

THE IMPACT OF A 360 FEEDBACK TOOL

The president of a private, family-owned wholesale plant nursery, one of the largest in California, was committed to learning and leading well. His management team was also family and employee focused, and the culture was centered around continually improving. To help improve their own leadership, the executive team decided to implement a new tool they had heard about and many companies were using: the 360 feedback tool. The tool was a survey where all of the managers asked for anonymous feedback on the survey form from their manager, peers, and direct reports, and the anonymous feedback would be shared with the manager. In theory, it sounded great. If team members received feedback about how to improve and followed through on it, it would mean progress for the person and the company, right? But what if something went terribly wrong?

Over a week, the managers received their feedback. The president, who was well-respected by his team and staff, also received his feedback. To everyone's surprise, he was devastated. For most managers, receiving the equivalent of a 95 percent rating was indicative of stellar leadership and a level that was rarely attained. But to this president, it was devastating. He believed he was doing better than "95 percent," and during the next few weeks and months, he was distressed and grieving. His team rallied around him to reassure him that the feedback was positive, that he was an excellent leader, and that they admired him. But no words brought him solace.

This 360 tool, although intended to be well-meaning, had an unpredictable and adverse impact. It left an emotional wound that was similar to a physical cut on the arm. The blood was gushing, and there didn't seem to be a way to stop the pain. The trauma that this company president and his team suffered was truly an eye-opener for all. It taught the team a powerful lesson about implementing a "management fad" without thinking through the possible consequences. The 360 tool was one that people believed could be helpful, but, upon deeper reflection and application, the organization came to see it as a mechanism for judging, criticizing, and blaming people instead. It diminished the president's pride and joy in his work. It took months and months for the team to heal together. The experience also taught the executives that if the president's feelings could be crushed with "constructive criticism," the employees had little chance of receiving feedback that could be useful to them.

In a similar situation, an executive team at a division of ITT was told by corporate HR to administer the 360 feedback tool. Everyone seemed excited about this new tool. Then the team saw its impact on their workers. The division had several hundred employees, many of whom had worked there for decades, from the time the company had been privately held. They were colleagues, supportive of each other at work, and many were friends outside of work. It was a lively, intense, fun, and hardworking culture. One particular production manager, Sally, was quite popular and a joy to work with. She always had a quick wit, an almost mischievous spirit, a dimpled smile, and blue eyes that sparkled. One day she received her 360 feedback from her manager, who was also her mentor. Sally was in tears. While the feedback and improvement ideas didn't seem jarring to the manager, Sally heard icy, cruel, and harsh criticism. She was shattered. Weeks and months went by. Her mentor was also devastated and felt helpless about how to repair the emotional damage to a great employee. I never saw Sally smile again. Her head was down, and her eyes were often teary. She still did her work without a complaint or a mistake. But the damage the 360 tool had on Sally had been done; the effect could not be reversed. Since the 360 survey feedback is anonymous, the impact it can have is even deeper; the recipient has no idea who has given the harsh critique. Was the critique to attack a person or was it well-meaning but had a devastating outcome? It can take only one anonymous comment, perhaps misunderstood or well-meaning but perhaps not thoughtful or caring, to hurt a person.

Words matter. Actions matter. But most important of all are the interactions, support, and care people have for each other. How do people show respect and work together to help each other accomplish their work and achieve their individual and collective goals? First, stop using fads, best practices, or "tools" that harm, especially if you feel it's justified because it's your job. It is not your job to harass, hurt, or bully people. It is your job to inspire and appreciate people.

EXAMPLE

Well-known for his writing and speaking out against performance appraisals, author Peter Scholtes once shared a story. "A CEO told me that he has a lot of dead wood in the company," Peter said. Peter then asked him, "Why did you hire live wood and kill it?" People come to work to do a good job. They take pride in their work. Leaders need to give them a good job to do. Leaders develop, mentor, and coach people to their fullest potential. They create an environment where employees experience joy in working to help others. On the other hand, micromanagers with too many of their own fears and control issues focus on judging, ranking, and rating people. Leaders that use performance appraisals tend to have a mindset of "power over" employees rather than "power with" employees. "Power over" creates an unfriendly, fearful work environment while "power with" unleashes creativity, energy, and drive.

LESSON

STOP administering performance appraisals. They are destructive, particularly those that rank and rate employees. They create internal competition and fear. They do not promote collaboration, teamwork, or the interconnected thinking that provides value for customers and stakeholders. More organizations are self-destructive due to the wrong leadership beliefs and policies that promote internal conflict. When leaders focus instead on developing and appreciating people, authentic collaboration and communication can flourish. Performance appraisal systems are full of wrong assumptions and practices that harm people and the success of an organization. As the Hippocratic Oath

taken by doctors and medical practitioners so simply and elo-
quently states: "Do no harm." Leaders in any organization might
learn from this lesson. Getting rid of grades, 360 surveys, and
performance appraisals may initially feel uncomfortable, as it
means giving up something you believed in and you're used to.
It is a change. But it is also a significant improvement, and ultimately, a transformation.

GETTING POOR RESULTS

QUESTIONS FOR YOU:

- Do you really understand why you lose customers and why they choose your competitor?
- What robust, dynamic system do you have that captures, shares, and effectively responds so that you can "wow" your customers?

Since the quality movement entered the United States in the 1980s, we have seen annual reports, ads, and now websites that espouse a focus on serving customers and valuing feedback. Yet companies have simultaneously experienced a sharp decline in having robust customer service teams available to serve customers. Consumers experience long wait times to make flight reservations, to ask a question at the insurance company, or for technical support that has often been outsourced abroad. When we do provide survey feedback or write a letter with a complaint or an idea for improvement, we may receive a form letter or a one-way e-mail in response. However, in either case, there is no name or return contact information. The e-mail is automatically sent and signed by "Mary." To contact "Mary" again with a follow-up question or comment is a dead-end.

Promises for customer service and desires for company feedback become empty words and platitudes. Often, even when organizations do receive *valued feedback*, little to no changes are implemented in the system to make a difference for the next customer. A renewed focus and leadership mindset for excellent quality and providing value would easily allow a few organizations to excel in their industry. The others who do not genuinely serve customers with quality will not survive. It's a choice that leaders make. Survival is optional. To survive, leaders to need to pivot; they need to disrupt their current thinking and take action to transform themselves and their organizations.

—

The global economy challenged the health and viability of many businesses and organizations. But too many poorly led and badly managed organizations use "a bad economy" or "unfair competition" as their excuse for less-than-optimal business results. Unless the economy is in a severe recession or depression, poor results may have nothing to do with the economy. Whether it's a good or bad economy, an executive team can watch its business decline and make excuses all the way to closing the doors. Or bold leaders can disrupt and innovate their own thinking and transform their business and capture new markets. There's that choice again: fail or survive.

What seems to take more businesses into decline is leadership arrogance: the executives "know a lot" or "know it all." Whether their enterprise has been alive for five, twenty, fifty, or one hundred years, it couldn't possibly fail. Or could it? Management can continue to struggle, to flounder, to be stuck in chaos, but they have a long list of reasons (or excuses) and don't ask for help. Generally, they stay focused on the bottom line. But it's the wrong focus, and it won't help them lead, transform, capture new markets, or turn around.

Poor management often fails to make a drastic and immediate commitment to question their organization's current beliefs, assumptions, and practices. They rarely learn a different way to improve, lead, and work together; to accelerate their engagement with their customers; and/or to identify and pursue new markets. Leaders do those things. That's what it takes to survive. It's a choice: flounder and fail or survive.

EXAMPLE

The airlines have been an easy target for customer complaints for at least the past two decades. There has been a continual shake-out with mergers and buyouts and failures in the industry. Some airlines hunkered down and treated their employees badly who, in turn, treated the customers badly. Other airline executives genuinely focused on the customer experience and quality, listened to their employees and customers, and have often maintained their profitability and expanded, even during challenging economic times.

As a road warrior of business travel and a passionate explorer of forty countries so far and almost all fifty states, I have racked up more than five million miles in air travel. For more than a decade, I was most loyal to American Airlines (even though almost every one of their tickets was at least $50 more than any other airline). My frequent flier mileage account showed more than three million miles, and I became a lifetime Platinum flyer and was well taken care of. Ten years ago, American Airlines's service suddenly and drastically declined, their routes diminished, the lack of training was evident based on their personnel's absence of attention to the customers, and the complaints skyrocketed. A new CEO (and then another and another) took the helm, and their words about caring about customers seemed genuine. And that's where the words stopped, serving as temporary bandages to the real issues at hand. Quality customer service was at an all-time low.

I began collecting data. For example, I noticed that when I flew on American, thirty-four out of thirty-five times the flight attendants did not greet the passengers with a hello, thank you, or good-bye at the end of the flight. (How much would that have cost?) Instead, they were preoccupied with talking to each other and complaining about the airline! If passengers asked for help, they received a dirty look. American was then financially hurting and showing regular losses. With metrics in hand, I wrote to the new CEO and shared my observations. I don't write often to CEOs, but I felt that the three or four issues I raised, supported with some hard data and my reputation of being a loyal premier flyer, would get someone's attention. Wrong assumption! A few months later, I received an unsigned form letter with no contact information defending their poor service!

Would they be your airline of choice? My associates and I stopped flying American unless we had absolutely no other way to get into a city. Periodically (every few years), I fly them again, but the quality of service is still lacking. The comparison is that some of the high quality, profitable airlines such as Jet Blue and Southwest (and there are more that are just not in my regular travel path, so I can't comment) have happy, dynamic, well-trained employees who engage with the passengers. If one attendant does not connect with the customers, it is rare, and I'm hoping they're just having a bad flight and will sleep it off and be ready to fly the next day. I thoroughly enjoy flying with them.

No organization is safe from failing. In fact, it's relatively easy to fail. It all starts with a lack of leadership without a compelling purpose (no, the purpose is not to make money; that's an outcome!). Leaders need to create a system, but several major airlines' systems are broken and need to be fixed. Some executives do not know how to fix a broken system and are totally out of touch with their customers. When leadership focuses on quality and continual improvement as key business strategies, they have an opportunity for success.

Management teams who lack leadership thinking will be short-term thinkers. They turn to making staff cuts, reducing training programs for employees, freezing hiring and travel, or fail to implement necessary change. They ignore the messages and concerns of their customers. In the words of Dr. Gluckman, and, as I mentioned in the Introduction, just like a large dinosaur, it may take a long time for this major airline or any large corporation to come to its knees. But its demise is certain if leaders do not personally focus on the essential elements of success and transformation. The question for floundering leaders is, "Are you not aware, or do you not care?"

—

There is a price to pay for poor quality and service. In many cases, CEOs, executives, and even managers are so far removed from the customer that each individual customer seems unimportant. Let's scale the example down to one that's familiar to all of us, as it illustrates the view from the other side of the table.

EXAMPLE

When you first move to a new area, you have many decisions to make about where you will take your business. You make choices. Those choices are based on reviews or getting referrals from Yelp or new neighbors or colleagues. One critically important choice to make is which local doctor you will see when you get sick. Let's examine the experience at two different doctors' offices.

You show up at your first appointment. The waiting room is crowded; the receptionist has you stand in front of her and wait to check in while she's answering phone calls and making copies. Then you sit and wait for thirty minutes, and you are informed that the doctor is a little behind schedule. Eventually, your name is called, and a nurse takes you to a private room, takes your vital signs, and tells you the doctor will be there soon. If it weren't for her nametag, you wouldn't even know her name. Finally, the doctor makes it to your room and introduces himself while he washes his hands with his back facing you. He rushes through his questions for you and writes you a prescription for a medication you've never heard of. If you have any problems, you're advised to come back in two weeks.

Not likely. This office decided to cut costs by cutting support staff and trying to rush more patients through a system that is already too backed up. You leave the office hoping the medication will make you feel better, but you definitely don't feel as though your doctor genuinely cares for your health. You will not return.

You plan a follow-up visit with another doctor. When you walk into the office, the assistant greets you, uninterruptedly takes down your information, gives you a booklet describing the health-care philosophy of this doctor's office, and tells you "The doctor will be with you shortly." Within minutes, a nurse comes out to the waiting room and brings you to the patient room. He thanks you for waiting, introduces himself, explains what he is doing as he takes your vitals as well as your blood pressure, and details its significance. He asks you to describe your symptoms and to clarify a few when he's not sure what you mean. He explains that Dr. Smith will be in soon and wishes you the best. When Dr. Smith arrives, she shakes your hand and introduces herself. After a full checkup, she explains your condition, what medicine she will give you, and how long it should be before you feel better. You leave already feeling better. Both doctors are coping with the high costs of running a medical practice, but this one decides to do it in a different way. She hires and trains more support staff in order to more effectively process patients and billing. Her patients feel respected, leave happy, and are sure to come back. She now has to spend much less money on recruiting new patients because her patients are comfortable and secure coming back to her.

How does your business compare? Do you cut costs at the expense of your customers? If you are fortunate enough to have a strong customer base, make sure you're not too far away to hear their opinions, and don't be afraid to make changes. Customers are important, and how they feel based on the quality of their experience with you can be just as vital as the product you deliver to them.

LESSON

STOP making excuses for results you don't like. Leaders create and build the organization. Only leadership can be accountable for its direction; the communication needed to clarify the direction and how people can contribute to it; the systems and process flow and their results; and, the quality, service, and the experience the organization delivers to its customers. Only leadership is accountable for building the system to achieve an effective connection between the company and being responsive with the customers.

The commitment and courage of leaders is needed to expect new experiments, to try new methods, and celebrate the efforts. Each one is a step closer to success. Without new experiments, leaders maintain the status quo.

Leaders have opportunities to experiment, improve, and ultimately create the system for their team to be self-motivated enough to contribute. Leaders create the possibilities for learning, working, and improving together.

SEARCHING FOR "BEST PRACTICES"

QUESTIONS FOR YOU:
- Are you a leader in your industry? Do others look to you for "best practices?"
- Do you spend more energy searching for "best practices" or innovating?

"Best practice" has become a commonly used term in past years to describe the most efficient and effective way to accomplish a task or procedure. Organizations are always on the lookout for "best practices" they can replicate and implement, but just the phrase "best practices" alone sets up unrealistic expectations throughout the organization, from the top down. Some proper terms an organization that wants to improve, innovate, and survive could use include "better" or "new" or "different" practices, meaning that the organization's leadership is continually striving to develop. The collective energy then shifts from complacent to dynamic.

Best practices—or employing a practice another organization has used to solve a problem—are often sought in an effort to save time. The "best practice" method is considered efficient to help accomplish work and get desired results. One company might research how other companies pay their salespeople, implement their rewards system, or recruit star employees, and try to introduce the same practices into their own organization.

However, chasing "best practices" and benchmarking what other organizations do often leads to stagnant thinking and copying. In their book *Rework,* Jason Fried and David Heinemeier Hansson discuss the dangers of this:

> "Unfortunately, copying in the business arena is unusually more nefarious. Maybe it's because of the copy-and-paste world we live in these days. You can steal someone's words, images, or code instantly. And that means it's tempting to try to build a business by being a copycat.
>
> That's a formula for failure, though. The problem with this sort of copying is it skips understanding—and understanding is how you grow. You have to understand why something works or why something is the way it is. When you just copy and paste, you miss that. You just repurpose the last layer instead of understanding all the layers underneath."[2]

A better practice, a better way to do something for one team is a misnomer for others. A best practice for one team or company will wreak havoc on another team. It doesn't fit or work.

Too many people think, "Oh good, we've found a best practice. It is the new industry standard." Managers of an organization will often accept the new practice for months, years, or even decades. They adopt an industry "best practice" and use it over and over without asking essential questions: "Does it help us achieve our aim?" "Does it solve our issues and work in our culture?" and "Does it serve our customers?"

Accepting a best practice removes the questioning, thinking, and experimenting that you need to align with the needs of your own organization and customers. Developing and implementing your own process focuses your team on engaging in and developing their own culture focused on continual learning, improvement, and innovation.

In the English language, the adjective "good" evolves to "better" and then finally, its superlative form, "best." We might say the service at a restaurant is good. During our next visit there it is better. If it is the best, it is as good as it gets. By definition, it can't get better. The focus is not on making it better. But if organizations are going to improve, if they're going to survive, they must understand that there is no "best" practice. The focus needs to be on continual improvement, not getting to the best practice and being finished with the focus on improving.

Many organizations comb through industry data so they can compare and benchmark themselves with the competition. They search for "best practices" that they can adopt in a hurry. They attend conferences to hear case studies and try to integrate and copy what others are doing, assuming their "best practices" will dovetail into their own systems well.

The pursuit of "best practices" is a poor replacement for leadership. It is important to be aware of what the competition and the industry are doing, and what lessons there are to learn, so you don't reinvent the wheel each time you need to solve a problem. However, leadership's job is to scan the environment and be aware of barriers and opportunities in the market. Rather than spending precious time pursuing "best practices" and playing catch-up, leaders can create an environment where energy is spent improving, innovating, and discovering new ways to add more value for their customers.

"BEST PRACTICES" IN THE NAVY

Several years ago, I was invited to be the commencement speaker to address a group of Naval Intelligence officials. They had just completed an Executive Leadership program and wanted a speaker familiar with the corporate leadership perspective. Having worked with dozens of Fortune 1000 corporations, I knew that I wanted to prepare a presentation that was both powerful and tangible. Fortunately, the group was a small class of forty students, allowing me to make the session intimate, robust, and interactive. After a brief introduction, I said, "My aim is to provoke your thinking. Much of what you may have learned over the past weeks will not be helpful or useful to you if you want to lead into the future." I wanted to make them uncomfortable, and curious. Next, I shared a list of common "best practices" being used in corporations and asked if any of these were being implemented in the naval intelligence world. Practices such as benchmarking, Lean Six Sigma, performance appraisals, incentives... were they using these there, too? Their hands shot up. They proudly nodded that they, too, were using some of the same practices. I calmly said, "I have one request: Stop." The audience was slightly puzzled. Why did I want them to stop? They had just spent a few weeks learning about these "best practices" currently being used by American corporations and other enterprises. I shared with them how, over several decades, I'd seen hundreds of these current "best practices" and management fads create working environments full of toxic behaviors, fear, internal competition, lack of collaboration, greed, arrogance, poor quality, complexity, and lack of productivity.

After the presentation, to which many did not know how to respond, the naval captain spoke. "It makes sense," he said. "We cannot lead if our thinking is in automatic pilot and we accept any management fad that is tossed in our In Basket. We have to think about what we are doing, why we do it, and the ramifications of adopting new practices and processes. Thank you for the challenge."

If you hear an idea and adopt it because it seems popular or easy, beware—it might be easy for only the short-term. When it stops working, the hard work that didn't get done earlier still has to be done. The issue must then be solved by brainstorming ideas, experimenting with various processes, and working diligently to improve them.

EXAMPLE

How often has one of your executives gone to a conference, heard of some trendy "best practice" the successful companies are using, and decided to implement it at your company, too? Employees suffer at the expense of a practice that doesn't work. The constant changing of "best practices" confuses employees and destroys productivity. Instead, people working together to continually improve will help boost morale, productivity, and profits.

LESSON

STOP pursuing and copying "best practices." We can have a "better" practice, a dynamic practice that is continually improving. But a "best practice" is a misnomer. It implies that the end has been reached and that there is no room for change. As the evolution of the word "good" implies, there's good, there's better (continually improving), and there's "best." "The best" means we're done improving, but continual improvement is exactly what we need.

CREATING INEFFECTIVE MISSION STATEMENTS:

QUESTIONS FOR YOU:
- Is your mission engaging and memorable?
- Does it communicate a compelling purpose that people can believe in?
- Does everyone in your community understand how they fit in and can contribute to that purpose in a way that makes a difference?

One of the first steps in traditional strategic planning processes is to create a mission statement. I want to emphasize this step because of the number of hours I've seen wasted in creating mission statements—hours that could be invested differently. The process often begins with brainstorming words, phrases, and ideas, and then assigning a few people the task of "word-smithing" them into some cohesive piece of communication that will guide the enterprise.

Many mission statements—or mission paragraphs, as they often turn out to be—sound similar from one organization to another: "We'll deliver the greatest products, be excellent, and provide great customer service." Sound familiar—and boring? Instead, discover what is at the heart of your organization. Ask: "What is your compelling purpose? What is your reason for being?" Once the compelling purpose is defined from the heart, people can engage together and commit to their work. The compelling purpose should be an organization's central mission, not a string of trivial buzzwords. All individuals can learn how they can contribute, add value, and work together to achieve a meaningful purpose. Relevant work will evolve over and over, but if a company is unified by an overlying purpose, it can adapt to a changing environment while maintaining its core values. Together a team can improve and innovate.

Once the compelling purpose or aim is defined and the direction of the organization clarified, leaders can communicate why this aim is essential throughout the organization. But what often happens is that the communication about what to do, how to achieve success, where the organization is going, who it's serving, and how progress will be measured is ineptly addressed. When an enterprise has a purpose, it must also have a system of communicating and diffusing the meaning of that purpose. Leaders communicating effectively use a system of communication diffusion. It is an essential foundation for effective communication about the organization and all it is attempting to achieve.

A system must be created for leadership to ensure that the key parts of the organization are communicating effectively with each other to accomplish the organization's central aim. The voice of leadership articulates the purpose of the organization "a hundred times a day." In every interaction—with peers, customers, vendors, staff, and partners—the leaders repeat and clarify the aim of the organization. Leaders help everyone and every team understand how to add value and contribute to achieving a larger aim for the organization, and for society at large. Inspiring leaders live out the organization's purpose. They embody it as if it is their own—and it may be! As a result, employees and partners begin living the purpose, too. Inspiring leaders genuinely care about their organization's compelling purpose and about the people who will help them achieve it.

EXAMPLE

School district leaders met for their annual off-site meeting to prepare for the school year. Once again, they began the meeting with reviewing their mission statement. They selected words to mash together to make the sentences of a paragraph that they could post all over the school. The process activated a heaviness and a sense of lethargy in the room.

A shift needed to occur. I asked a critical question that seemed foreign at first: "What is your compelling purpose?" Repeatedly I asked the same question slowly and let the group process it. Responses came as guesses accented by quizzical looks. I probed further, "Why do you exist? Why are you here? What inspired you to pursue this profession? Where is your passion? Is the compelling purpose of the school district to test and measure and discipline and frighten and bore students?"

Finally, they reached their epiphany: it was *joy in learning* that became their unified mantra. What if the entire school district was inspired with the purpose of creating joy in learning? Would the school superintendent, school nurse, teacher, janitor, and first-grade child be able to understand and articulate the purpose? Could they each understand how they could contribute toward it? Could they work together to accomplish it? For example, the janitor understands that his role is not limited to emptying trash and cleaning floors. Rather, he is proud to create a clean, safe environment where children can experience joy in learning. He is proud of his work and of his contribution to the school's purpose.

Their focus on adapting a new way of learning and leading together was a paramount step in their transformation journey. Their epiphany opened their eyes to new meaning in education and new roles they would adopt and support each other in to attain joy in learning. They all had contributions to make. The school district leaders and those in the school community knew that transforming the way they had been thinking and acting would be their new strategy going forward. They would continue to learn together and develop plans, systems, processes, and a culture where everyone in the district could make a difference in children's lives.

—

The quality and quantity of questions that leaders ask throughout an organization are directly linked to the organization's success. Employees' overall level of communication, meaningful interaction, and understanding is linked to this success, as well. An effective organization functions better when everyone is working in a way that reflects the organization's core values.

EXAMPLE

Howard Miller, senior vice president of operations at a large television network, initiated a new project, with a cross-functional team, to better serve their broadcast customers' needs. He gathered a group of about twenty managers and staff from across the company to have their first conversation, and he launched the project meeting. As the management consultant and facilitator, I asked the question, "What do you want to accomplish?" Around the table each person responded differently—but many of the answers were self-serving. Immediately the group began to discuss ideas, flounder, take sides, jockey for a power position, and fail. With their independent thinking, failure was off to a good start. Howard had assumed (wrongly) that there was a shared understanding about the project and how it fit into the company's purpose and strategic business initiatives. There was not.

Quickly realizing that this flaw could lead to the group's failure in accomplishing the goals that the company needed accomplished, I proposed a new question: "What do you want to accomplish *together?*" The addition of one word, "together," offered a significant shift in how the group needed to think, communicate, and work. They learned that they *first* needed to agree on what they wanted to accomplish. Otherwise they each would be working from their own personal perspective, rather than the team perspective. They would not see the larger picture and the common aim. They would not see how they could individually contribute to achieve it. Once they were in agreement as to the aim, they could move to the next step: defining by what method they would *achieve* the aim.

LESSON 1

STOP creating meaningless mission statements. Leaders must have an aim for their enterprise. If there is no compelling purpose that people care about and can contribute to, they will work to serve their own self-interests.

LESSON 2

The compelling purpose of the organization must be exciting, sustainable, and communicated endlessly times one hundred throughout, so everyone understands why they should believe in its direction and how they can contribute to achieving it. Simplify for clarity, so that as the message is relayed, it does not change or lose its significance. A coherent understanding of the aim is critical. If people do not agree on the purpose and direction of the enterprise, it will move like a boat in muddy water. Until the direction is agreed upon and clear to everyone, do not embark on the methods for implementation. Agreement and engagement— not merely consensus—are key. Be aware of consensus-building, or people coming to agreement for the sake of consensus and then moving on. Consensus often breeds mediocrity, and mediocrity is not part of an organization that has a compelling aim, is continually improving, or is innovating. Move forward with the aim only when it is compelling! If you move forward with strategies before people understand and are engaged, implementation will flounder, and you'll end up back at the compelling aim discussion again.

Mission statements are often static and made up of meaningless rhetoric. By the time the words are strung together, they lack meaning, focus, and do not provide direction. But by answering the simple questions, "What is your compelling purpose? Why do you exist?" an innate and powerful vision, with the connection to a better future, can be defined. People can continually move forward, adapt, and respond in an evolving, dynamic direction that serves all customers.

When creating a compelling purpose or aim, it is imperative to keep it simple. The aim answers the questions of, "What are we trying to accomplish together? Why is this direction important?" Do not mix in the question of "Who are we serving?" Instead, keep the aim clear and simple. The first and most powerful step in succeeding is to be very clear about the purpose, so everyone understands it and how they are integral to making it happen. Everyone contributes toward it. From this, the "how" and "who" questions can be answered.

Note, if an aim is complex and unclear, the methods to achieve it will flounder and consume time. The aim will have to be readdressed, so it is best to be sure it is clear before proceeding to achieve your aim.

KEY TAKEAWAY

Essentially, this STOP means both redefining and rethinking the meaning of the mission statement, and recreating it with a different process. I've observed hundreds of teams working on mission statements the same way they've done them year after year. Sometimes, they even pull out their notes from the previous year. To drive bold, important improvements, the thinking and the process needs to transform. Instead of arriving at a mission by choosing interesting words from a dictionary and trying to mush them together, think about how your organization needs to be different, bold, engaging, meaningful, and focused, and can have an impact to those you serve like never before. Make your message crisp, short, and memorable. Then, focus on answering deeper questions, like, "How will our work be meaningful to those we serve? How will it take us into the future?"

A murky mission statement or paragraph is archaic. But a compelling aim that is well communicated and engaging is a catalyst for people to evolve *together*, achieve dreams, and create futures and possibilities for others. Test your aim. Is it compelling, memorable, succinct, and will it bring people together to make a difference?

CREATING ROAD MAPS

QUESTIONS FOR YOU:
- Do you have a road map and know specifically where you are going?
- Are you creating a new future: improving, innovating, and adapting?
- Hint: Leaders don't create road maps.

When executives want to meet goals and targets and to grow profits, they encourage their teams to work on a "road map" to get "there." Too often, senior executives think they will get to the next level by using a road map. The thinking is wrong; the direction is wrong. Therefore, the goals or growth they want to achieve are never realized.

I want to take a trip from San Francisco, California to Phoenix, Arizona. I know where I am, and I know where I want to go. It is easy to use a road map to look at my options and decide how to get there. If I decide to fly, I can even "map" out my plans, even if I do so only in my head. I can choose whether to use a taxi or limousine service or drive to an airport, or ask a friend to drop me off. I can use the San Jose, San Francisco, or Oakland airport; I have a choice of airlines, flight times, and fares. Whether flying or driving, I can use a "map" because I am going from point A to point B, and both of them already exist.

However, if I am a leader and I want to help my organization grow to a new level, accelerate sales and profits, innovate, and transform to a place we've never been before, a road map is of no use. The road map doesn't exist because there is no point B. We haven't been there. If we create an arbitrary point B (increase sales by 5 or 10 percent), we may achieve it, but we might have actually been able to increase sales by 22 percent—how could we have known? Once we created a numerical goal, we're psychologically programmed to slow down our efforts when we got close to it—it's basic human behavior.

If a road map is useless for growth, what do we use? Modern pioneers use a compass and anticipate as they continually gather

STRATEGIC COMPASS

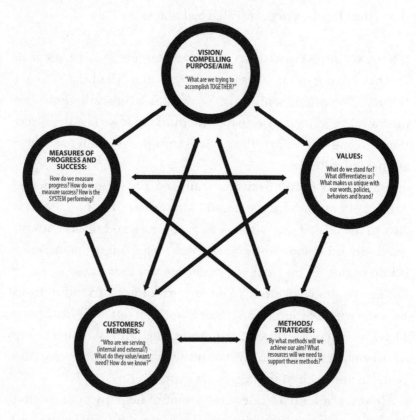

and assess new knowledge to decide which direction they will go and how. Leaders use a strategic compass (explained in detail in Part Three) for the same reason. It's a tool that lets them learn and adapt.

EXAMPLE

As a young leader, Frank, the company president, learned the importance of anticipating. He ran a chain of car dealerships in Hawaii and California. In the cutthroat automobile dealership industry, the fight for customers could be especially fierce. And if the auto product is bad, it does not matter how good the selling process is—the vehicle sits in inventory. What could Frank's team do to innovate? First, they committed to studying and applying the philosophy of Dr. W. Edwards Deming. His principles gave them a strong theoretical foundation from which to begin.

Frank's team prepared to open a seventh auto dealership. At that time, they adopted an approach that was totally different and innovative in the auto industry. Before the dealership opened, all of the employees were educated in quality principles that focused on continually improving their service to customers and supporting each other. They worked together to create the processes so that from the time a customer walked in the door until they drove off with their new car, they experienced consistent, high-quality service. Instead of hiring salespeople, Frank's team hired people with specific experience in customer service. They were one of the first auto dealerships in the nation to implement the policy of not negotiating the car's sale price. It was transformation in action. The customers loved the experience. Within a few months, hundreds of cards and letters of appreciation were posted on the bulletin board in the showroom. The team's energy was contagious, and sales steadily increased.

LESSON

STOP assuming that concrete numerical goals, targets, and road maps will create your future success. Leaders must shift their thinking and use a strategic compass to continually adapt to customers' changing needs. As technology strategist Dan Burrus suggests, "Create a new market and have it all to yourself."

The road map approach is useful if you know where you are and where you are going. But it is only useful for the short term. If I'm going to the grocery store or to San Diego for the weekend, that's relatively easy to plan. If I'm going on a trip around the world for six months, I can choose my direction and plan to some extent, but after that, the ability to adapt will play a key role.

To have a vision and a tentative plan for the future also means building a system that can help your plan become a reality. What are all of the parts that must come together for the trip to be a success? Varied elements are essential for an organization to progress into the future, and each one is different. The key is to have the conversations with your key stakeholders about what you need and how all the parts are going to work together to create that success. Begin to work the plan, and then adapt as you learn and continue to move forward.

USING THE LANGUAGE OF FAILURE

- What is the vocabulary that leaders and robust teams use?
- What are the words and tone that leaders use in your organization?

Vocabulary makes a difference. It is a powerful reflection of a leader's or group's or culture's thinking. It is the window into the mind. It is an organizing principle, and it is also the guide to the behaviors that follow. If a leader models powerful, thought-provoking rhetoric, and is repeatedly open to challenging the organization's norms, employees will also match that style of thinking and the behaviors that are aligned.

EXERCISE

There are two companies that we'll go visit together. One is the Lock Company. We enter and are given a tour. As we ride along on our golf cart, we hear snippets of people's conversations, and observe the work environment:

Cut costs

Lay low

Hushed whispers

Locked file cabinets (inside are the plans and charts and data)

Losses

Manipulate the data

Stress

Ethics

Vulnerable

That's the way we've done it
    here for twenty years

Blame

We can outlast them and this
    program, too

Dirty carpet, dated furniture,
    coffee stains on the
    counter tops, vending
    machines, tall cubicles
    with quiet workers facing
    their computers, piles of
    documents

Reduce

Eliminate

Fear

Rank and rate people

Mistakes

Don't rock the boat

I'm babysitting; they act like
    kindergarteners

There's not enough
    individual accountability

Why change?

Layoffs

We're losing market share

Poor economy is the reason

What's wrong with the way
    we've been doing it?

Wait and see

The holiday party is
    cancelled

Change

Crush the competition

CYA

Sure, I said yes in the
    meeting, but no way; they
    don't know what they're
    talking about

We don't need any new ideas

Misalignment

The employee lunchroom is
    sparse and dirty

It was a typical company
    tour: workers work, and
    many stop to stare before
    looking away or kicking a
    crumbled piece of paper
    under the desk

On Wednesday, we visit the Defining Point Company. Guided by our host, we hear words and phrases as we experience and observe another organizational environment:

Hardly anyone is sitting at his or her desk

Groups of people are engaging in robust conversations in small conference rooms or along the hallway walls looking at the process flowcharts

Wow

Opportunities

What do we need to accomplish together?

Three different teams of five people are in intense discussions along a process flowchart that is mounted on the wall and extends the length of the hallway

How can we?

Provocative

Possibilities

Laughter

Fresh

I like that

What if we...?

Explore

Fun

Joy in work

Learning, training, and education

Serve the customers

Catalyst for change

Our compelling purpose

Embrace uncertainty and create the future

Lessons learned...let's keep improving

Innovation

Curious

Unique

Bold

Take risks

Management is prediction

Let's let the process run and look at the data over time, no tampering

The lunchroom for all employees is clean and well stocked

Both the Lock Company and the Defining Point Company are hiring. Both have openings in your discipline. They could use a new CEO or plant manager or engineer or accountant. After having read the previous chapters, you know to be wary of work environments that focus on quotas, cost cutting, and incentives, rather than improving processes and relationships; work that happens in silos rather than in team-oriented environments; and work that focuses on blame and criticism rather than inspiration and development. You also know that successful organizations are run by leaders who embrace high quality, continual improvement, innovation, serving customers, collaboration in action, investing in their employees, and are accountable for the systems they create.

Where will you apply?

LESSON

An old world uses "best practice" language. Its black-and-white thinking leads to struggles, poor morale, and failure. A better world encourages innovative thinking, fostering a culture full of opportunities, possibilities, and continual improvement, and working *together* for a common aim.

OLD WORLD	A BETTER WORLD
Black or white	Full of color
Best	Better or worse, continually improving
Change	Improve
Rules and compliance structure	Options and possibilities
Right or wrong	Various perspectives to consider
No or yes only	Maybe
Final, done	Adaptable, agile
Finite	More or less
I can't	"How can we?"
Stuck	Forward
Adversarial and competitive	Supportive and collaborative
Win-lose thinking	Win-win-win thinking
Focus on the results and bottom line	Focus on the processes *and* the results

SUMMARY OF PART ONE

- STOP common practices that are "bad practices" disguised as "best practices."
- STOP doing things that harm people and put organizations into decline, either slowly or quickly.
- Shift the mindset and reactive behaviors of cost cutting, laying off, hunkering down, and going numb with fear to new thinking focused on building better systems and processes and communication and trust. That is the thinking that will drive new behaviors.
- Challenge the belief that executives are doing the right thing and doing it well.

Leaders commit to stopping the practices I describe in Part One because they become aware. They realize that those practices are actually harming people, productivity, and profits, and sending their organizations into decline. The questions begin to emerge, slowly at first, and then more rapidly. One company president said, "If I so strongly believed in ranking, rating, and judging people through performance appraisals, and then I realized the devastation that performance appraisals are wreaking throughout this company, what else might I be wrong about?" Only leaders who are open to learning and don't get defensive or overconfident can transform and make a positive, profound difference.

The profound questions! The huge AH-HAs! Personal transformation! They are all the foundation for transforming any organization, corporation, or education, healthcare, or environmental system. Personal transformation begins with challenging our own beliefs and assumptions. When people join organizations, they often mistake the use of "worst practices" for "best practices." In most cases, organizations adopt "best practices" unintentionally (though there are some exceptions). The flaw in the system occurs when some member of leadership believes in the direction of the "status quo" and doesn't think about the real outcomes and consequences the current systems deliver.

One can wonder: why has greed and arrogance become so prevalent in our executive teams and boards of directors that they will risk even jail time for the almighty dollar? Why do teens cheat in high school or college? Why do they jump in front of trains when the stress from the internal competition the school system creates is more than their young lives can bear? Why?

What do we do next? If we stop wasting time and energy on creating poor systems that deliver ugly outcomes and incentives, if we stop ranking and rating people and holding individuals accountable before we take a close look at our organizational structure, if we stop chasing "best practices" and if we stop continually reorganizing without understanding why, what do we do in place of those things? As author Peter Scholtes once said, "If you know that smoking is bad for you and you decide to stop, do you look for something else to stick in your mouth and light on fire?" If you need to stop doing something because you have learned it will hurt you and others around you, just stop. Do not replace bad practices; just let them go. When you stop, you will find you possess an entirely new energy.

Leadership is accountable for creating a system that provides profound knowledge to its organization. Are you a leader providing your system what it needs to function effectively? The system needs to work, yet also be able to adapt. Leaders who create and build a system also need to ensure that it has the support, resources, and focus for improvement and innovation required for it to thrive. Survival is optional. If the system does not have the foundation that it needs, it will flounder and fail.

The power of Part One is that it illustrates beliefs, thinking, practices, and behaviors that are barriers to healthy growth. Leaders need to STOP these. Leaders who try to change or improve by adding new practices on top of the old might as well be putting fresh strawberry jam on moldy bread.

STOP the old thinking and challenge yourself about what needs to be done to accomplish your aim. Wipe the slate clean and start with a fresh mindset.

The Bold and Fearless Thinking That Leaders Must START

Psychology DISRUPT
Systems Purpose
Optimize Question
Strategies Scan PIVOT
Diversity Knowledge Diffuse
Ask Listen
Behaviours People Commit
Connect
Variation LEARN Adapt
Build Communicate
Theory

■ INTRODUCTION ■

Part Two illustrates what we need to start thinking and doing differently.

In this section, we will:

- Examine leadership transformation.
- Adopt new leadership thinking that will lead to better behaviors and actions.
- Embrace courage from deep within.
- Explore a systematic management philosophy with a theoretical foundation (rather than the latest fads).
- Innovate and adapt in a culture of cooperation.

TRANSFORMATION IN ACTION

"Profound knowledge comes from the outside and by invitation only."
—Dr. W. Edwards Deming

Theories are often shunned in the real world of work. People are not interested in the conceptual when the day-to-day focus is on what we do, what we measure, who is accountable, who is the best, and, ultimately, bottom line results. People are often so busy focusing on details or quotas that they have little time to think about what they are doing, why they are doing it, and for whom. They forget to think about the big picture and the greater purpose they serve to their team, to the organization, and to their customers. To run a sustainable organization, leaders must understand theory. Leaders create the system with a theoretical framework for running the organization, and employees contribute to the bigger picture. Those who can apply theory within their foundation can plan for the future and help their organization adapt with the changing climate. Business schools are often dropping theory classes and focusing on delivering one-year MBA programs. In this setting, students will learn "best practices" for the problems of today, but they will lack the theories to apply to solving the problems of tomorrow.

A theory of transformation means there will be a profound change in structure that creates something new. Leaders need a method for transformation. Transformation occurs through a system of interactions. Leaders must continually question, challenge, explore, discover, evaluate, test, and create. This process begins with the leader's realization that their organization's current thinking is inaccurate and often destructive. Leaders understand that in transformation, there is no destination, as the journey has never been traveled before. The process of successful transformation requires leaders who question, experiment, learn, and adapt well.

Again, an essential point is that leaders are accountable for creating the system whose parts interact and work. Employees are responsible for contributing to the system. But if the system is broken, the employees can't fix it. Leaders must fix it with the help of their employees.

A THEORETICAL FOUNDATION FOR TRANSFORMATION: A SYSTEM OF PROFOUND KNOWLEDGE

For leading transformation and taking your teams and organizations where they've never been before, Dr. W. Edwards Deming offered his management theory. He presented to his students and clients the System of Profound Knowledge (SoPK) as a new management lens. This lens is a different way to think about leadership and provides a theoretical foundation for management. The SoPK includes four interactive and interdependent parts: appreciation for a system, knowledge about variation, theory of knowledge, and theory of psychology. The lens is a new way to think that helps leaders create, build, and optimize a system (organization). The challenge is to use the lens without layering the new thinking on top of the "old way we've always been doing things."

The SoPK is a powerful theoretical foundation and a new management lens. In application, it must be effectively communicated. I've added to that a foundation for the SoPK to help leaders effectively communicate: The Theory of Communication

Communicating the SoPK

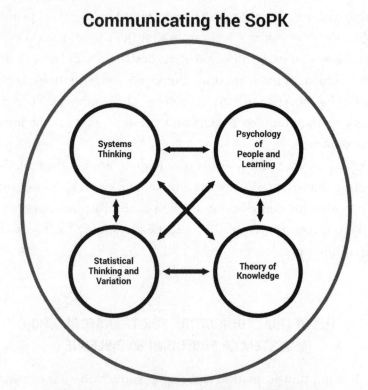

Theory of Communication Diffusion

Diffusion. Leaders must communicate the aim so everyone understands it. They must inspire other people to be clear about their own aims, processes, customer needs, and data (rather than opinions). And they must share their learning lessons. Without communication diffusion, the SoPK will be ineffective and sub-optimized.

It takes leadership with courage and the new knowledge (or lens) to transform an organization. Transformational leaders care deeply about developing people to their fullest potential and growing a healthy organization for the long term.

Leaders do not delegate the transformation work. Transformation is not project or program management or big data analysis. It is not strategic planning that can be delegated to a committee. This is not leading. These activities will not ensure that your organization improves, thrives, innovates, survives, or is sustainable. Instead, without leadership and direction, the silos and barriers will build up, and the culture will become dysfunctional and toxic.

THE JOB OF A GREAT LEADER

Great leaders know they cannot delegate their critical job. Great leaders must create a compelling purpose and direction, design and optimize a system to achieve their desired results, and develop an environment where people who are **self-motivated** have an insatiable appetite to contribute to the aim. Together they continually learn, improve, innovate, and deliver value to their stakeholders (whether they be customers, members, students, or patients) and new markets. Together the leaders will drive the organization to a whole new level of success.

People can live their lives to their fullest potential by learning, working, improving, and innovating TOGETHER. By helping the people around them in physical and virtual communities alike, and by embracing transformation, leaders can design better education systems that create joy in learning and working rather than conducting too many standardized tests or performance appraisals; leaders can design better health systems that focus on wellness and helping the ill rather than focusing on paperwork, bureaucracy, facing malpractice lawsuits, and insurance abuse; and leaders can create social systems that respect diversity, environmental systems that preserve the health of our planet for generations to come, and enterprises that promote the selling of valuable goods and services to satisfy customers' needs. Leaders have the capacity to do all of this when they have a new mindset, focus, and priorities.

Leaders who transform will START:

Developing Essentials for the Foundation to Grow
Developing Natural Leaders Who Transform
Creating a System for Optimization
Understanding Variation
Seeking Knowledge
Understanding People
Transforming, Not Merely Changing
Discerning Between the Three Different Kinds of Change

DEVELOPING ESSENTIALS FOR THE FOUNDATION TO GROW

LEADERS:

- Pursue learning about transformation and how to lead a transformation.
- Ask strategic questions that challenge the practices and structures you currently have in place.
- Explore thinking about how to innovate your leadership by looking through a radically new lens.
- Assume that your current beliefs and assumptions will lead your organization to fail. What would you need to do to save it? What if you started all over tomorrow with a startup to serve your customers?
- Gain strategic systems knowledge.
- Use statistical thinking to optimize the whole organization.
- Understand the psychology of people, as well as the psychology behind a creative, collaborative culture.
- Scan, plan, implement, and make decisions based on data in context.
- Communicate effectively.

Beliefs and knowledge are developed over time. If you want to rapidly challenge current beliefs, assumptions, and habits while also becoming more knowledgeable, it is helpful to have resources (at least the names of a few good books) or a teacher or mentor. If you have a coach, she should have a deep commitment to guiding and teaching a team, whether on the football field, battleground, or corporate offices.

Senior executives are wise *not* to hire consultants with whom they feel too comfortable and choose instead to bring on a coach who can give them an entirely new experience in transformation. Having a coach who can help you transform will be a new experience. A coach who possesses rare and profound knowledge will provoke and challenge leaders' strategic thinking and provide the guidance they need to through the implementation phase to effectively transform.

Leadership, and innovation in leadership thinking, requires many leaps of faith. It is not for the arrogant, overconfident, or greedy. It is for those who show they can and will make a difference—those who lead the shift in belief from, "I can't" to "How can we?" Transformative leaders are comfortable beginning the journey without envisioning the transformation at the end—because there is no end.

Can a company grow from $30 to $40 million, or will it surpass everyone's expectations, and the numerical goal set for it, and achieve $300 million? Can a company shift from $500 million to $2 billion and leapfrog the competition? Is it possible that the global nonprofit can survive and be sustainable for future decades? The answer is yes.

Transformation is profound. Leaders who commit to the journey have an ability to commit to the unknown. With profound knowledge, a commitment to staying open to new learning, and courage (it's not easy, but it is exhilarating), more and more unique, visionary, and often humble leaders are choosing to survive.

DEVELOPING NATURAL LEADERS
WHO TRANSFORM

What is the role of leadership? What philosophy of leadership do leaders need today, and in the future, to achieve a competitive edge? What leadership thinking and strategies accelerate progress and success, and what thinking or strategies lead to an organization's demise?

HOW CAN I BE A BETTER LEADER?

Twenty years ago, when I worked at a management consulting firm called Process Plus, the owner and my mentor, Dr. Perry Gluckman, received a call from one of our new clients, a man named Bill. Bill was a division manager for Dow Chemical, and he was going to be in town and wanted to have dinner. Perry had plans to be out of the state and volunteered me to go in his place. I was new at the firm and managing marketing and sales—a novice when it came to understanding leadership transformation and consulting. I had been diligently reading and studying about the leadership topics over the past weeks but had years to go before I'd feel that I had a strong foundation in the theories and applications.

I was extremely nervous to dine with a Fortune 500 executive (though he is a very nice man). We met at the restaurant at 7:00 p.m. After a few minutes of pleasantries and ordering drinks and appetizers, he posed the first question: "Marcia, how can I be a better leader?" To this day, I will never forget that question! I immediately knew I wanted to be somewhere else, anywhere else, but where I was. I thought to myself, "How in the world would I know? You are leading thousands of people, and I am leading no one! You would know better than I would." But I could tell he was sincere in his question, and it would be helpful if I took him seriously. Fortunately, the last ten books I had been reading and studying (all approved by Perry) were all books about leadership. I took a deep breath and began sharing some of the concepts that stood out to me from those ten books; our dialogue began, and we explored the topic of leadership for the next three hours. At some point, I must have become more relaxed, and our conversation progressed naturally. Soon after I arrived home, Perry called me from his travels and asked, "How was dinner?" My response was quick: "Don't ever have me do that again! I was a nervous wreck and don't know if I said anything that made sense." He asked about our conversation, which I summarized as best I could, and he said, "It sounds like it went very well." The client confirmed that he thought it was a most thought provoking conversation, and that he had found it helpful. "Yes!" I thought. Even Fortune 500 executives can benefit from hearing fresh perspectives.

We worked with that division manager and his staff for several more years, and we watched leadership knowledge develop in so many people on his team. Bill was committed to continually learning and improving himself, his leadership, and his listening. He learned from everyone around him, listened to their ideas, and studied the data over time and in context. Together, he and his team could make better, more informed decisions—though sometimes, of course, he would have to make tough ones.

DEFINING LEADERSHIP

Many organizations have too many projects, too few resources, too much internal competition for rewards, too little focus, and, most critically, too little understanding about how all the parts of the organization need to work together. Teams work to support the direction a company is going and to help accomplish the strategic goals and compelling purpose of the organization. But without a clear purpose and a methodology to accomplish it together, it doesn't matter how great the projects and people are, how hard everyone works, how efficient the processes might be, what "best efforts" and "best practices" are used, how much big data is analyzed, or how many defects Six Sigma analysis—a well-known application tool for statistical process control—reveals.

Leadership must be able to ask the hard questions and be open to new concepts. Without this desire to improve, a leader might be able to maintain a good organization, yet the system (the organization itself) can easily fail—and many do.

Leadership is not easy. It requires an ability to inspire people and to communicate effectively to engage them and harness their commitment to a purpose larger than themselves. It requires executives to have a new way of thinking and strive to cultivate knowledge and traits that are often uncommon in today's workplace, including:

- The courage to challenge bad practices such as short-term, bottom-line thinking, or slow, fear-based decision making.
- The knowledge to base decisions on data observed over time and in context.
- The patience and commitment to focus on innovating, to sustain the long-term health of an organization.

■ The compassion needed to create jobs instead of cutting costs through layoffs, grabbing the annual bonus, and abandoning the company.

Lead is a verb. Leading is a process that continually improves over time. Great leaders continually learn and engage in practices of self-discovery, self-development, and self-control. They have a vision for the long term and understand that their role is to transform. Leadership creates courage and authenticity creates trust.

Leadership requires that leaders pursue knowledge that challenges what is currently being taught in many of the "best" universities, by the "best" professors, churning out the "best" job candidates with the highest GPAs.

In reality, if we buy into the "best" mentality, our achievements will fall short and we will create win-lose strategies in work and life. Why do the "best" job candidates, "best" schools, "best" efforts, and "best" practices often lead our organizations, our projects, and our cultures into decline and dysfunction?

Simply and fundamentally: because of a lack of leadership knowledge. Leaders who cannot think beyond pre-established ideas and concepts won't be able to disrupt and transform themselves, their systems, their employees, or their organizations.

A PROFESSOR AND A ROOM OF HIGH-RANKING MILITARY OFFICERS

Recently, I was invited to sit in on a session on transformation and leadership being delivered to about thirty senior-ranking military officers who each had more than twenty-five years of service in a command position. The depth of the material was important; these officers created policies for war and managing the war machine and were responsible for hundreds of thousands of military and civilian lives.

I was anxious to discover what the top military minds in our nation would learn and discuss. The overseeing professor gave a short introduction, then gave them a specific assignment. "Break into teams of five," she said, "and then brainstorm the traits of a good leader. I'll give you twenty minutes, and then we'll discuss them." Was I in a dream—or a nightmare? This couldn't possibly be happening! Their time away from their troops and the Pentagon was precious, and this was how their next hour would be spent? After more than twenty-five or thirty years of leading, they were wasting their time in this elementary exercise. In the military world, they embody effective leadership; bad leaders don't make it to such a high rank (though inevitably, one or two who learn how to manipulate the system may slip through the cracks). I watched this activity unfold and thought how such an elementary exercise needed to be exchanged for one that engaged these leaders in robust, dynamic thinking and challenged them to consider what a leader needs to know to transform and design new systems. How would "creating a list of leadership traits" help these esteemed officers deliver and optimally create and lead a new system within the complex structure of the U.S. military? That is the challenge in a rapidly changing world, and these types of remedial activities inspire no one to innovate and transform.

We need leadership with the type of systems knowledge that is rarely understood and practiced today. Without this knowledge, executives and managers oversee individual departments, silos, and divisions without understanding that the whole is larger than the sum of many parts.

Let's think about a car. If we take the "best" parts from the Volvo, Mercedes, Lexus, Mini Cooper, and BMW and put them together, will we have a car that works? Of course not. This is why many organizations and projects fail. Some executives think that if they bring the "best" candidates from the "best" schools and use the "best" practices, they have the recipe for success. Instead, we have a sure recipe for internal competition, silos, and failure.

The systems and statistical knowledge (how people gather and analyze data and make decisions based on it in context) needed in organizations is rarely taught in our schools and universities. But if the knowledge needed for organizational success was readily available to leaders in all areas of education, government, and commerce, we would have committed people working together with a common aim and supportive resources, a strong and healthy worldwide economy, health care and education systems that serve people well, and a vibrant, sustainable environment and Earth.

THE ESSENTIAL QUALITIES AND COMPETENCIES OF A LEADER

So what exactly are we missing? Leadership requires:

- Knowledge based in a theoretical foundation of management.
- Systems and statistical thinking.
- Knowledge about people and how they learn, interact, and are motivated.
- The understanding that management is prediction; data presented over time and in context is better for decision making.
- A genuine commitment to rigorous and continual learning, especially at the executive level.
- Patience with chaos and upheaval, and the ability to facilitate solutions and manage the chaos and upheaval.

- Dedication to articulating the organization's direction well and repeatedly.
- Listening deeply, with perseverance and tenacity.
- Respect, understanding, and care for people.
- Courage and humility.

Leaders with these qualities can discern the difference between management fads and powerful transformation and can identify supporting processes and tools that can accelerate their organizations' progress. So how are you doing? Are you a leader? What is the legacy you will leave? What will your employees and customers say about your leadership and the ease with which you interact with your organization?

LEADERS TRANSFORM

Focused leaders work tirelessly to transform their organizations. They are adept at devising strategies that will allow them to improve, focus on quality, innovate, and commit to adding value and serving customers. Leaders build and guide a portfolio of interdependent projects and operations that lead to system optimization and a culture that delivers continual learning (the only hope for a competitive edge), progress, and success. They ask, "What? What if? How?" They never accept the status quo. They never fall into complacency, arrogance, or greed. They strive to be responsive. They identify fear in the organization and work relentlessly to reduce it and build trust.

In his book *The Anticipatory Organization,* author Daniel Burrus writes "Disruptor or Disrupted: You Have a Choice: Fighting to maintain the status quo instead of identifying and pursuing disruption will sink you deeper and deeper into a spiral of fruitless and frustrating reaction. When you struggle to protect and defend what you have, you only become further entrenched in your current business model and way of thinking—a position that can often lead to outright disaster."[3]

LEADERS BUILD

Success prevails when leaders build a foundation with a clear purpose and strategies, optimizing systems and processes, and a culture of collaboration. Leadership creates the strategies and operational planning, defines key business issues, and forms project and process improvement teams to do the work that will serve customers' needs.

What happens when teams do not understand the purpose they are trying to achieve together? Projects drag on and are late and over budget; employees become tired and frustrated; management panics and forces out "something" that doesn't meet customers' needs. The enterprise suffers from higher costs, greater inefficiencies, and poor quality and is sent into a spiraling decline.

LEADERS ENGAGE THE CUSTOMER

A Fortune 500 company recently lost a major contract with a client it had for more than twenty-five years. Project teams had diligently used project management metrics to track progress, but the company lacked engaged leaders who understood what the customer needed today and in the future. Even though the project metrics reflected the specific characteristics of the project, they didn't support the strategic goals of the company. Metrics tracking is no substitute for leadership.

A project group can, for example, track the number of technical manuals and documents it writes and the percentage of projects it completes on time, but these metrics don't tell us if the team is writing the content the customer needs, or writing it in a way the customer can easily use. What's more valuable: tracking the schedule, or spending time visiting the customer to understand how they use the product and what they will need in the future? (Keep in mind that it is our job, not the customer's job, to innovate.) Leadership must create a system that supports and serves customers.

ESSENTIAL MANAGEMENT PRINCIPLES

Organizations are facing more pressure to compete than ever before, and many leaders are confronting new challenges. Leaders who can draw upon a foundation of management principles that promote system optimization can adapt, respond, survive, grow, succeed, and create a new future. But most leaders do not have this knowledge, or the necessary experience.

Focusing on the bottom line, the results, and the stock price destroys organizations. Those that guard their fundamental principles of serving customers by continually improving quality are those that are choosing to survive. Those who chase management fads give up that choice and often flounder and fail.

Of course, leaders are aware of the numbers (revenues, profits, share price, etc.). Those are part of the system, but there's variation in everything. Numbers go up and down. The real news would be if the numbers stayed the same, but they always fluctuate. Leaders with profound knowledge understand the theory of variation, trends, and multiple causes so they don't react and tamper with the processes. Do you react and tamper on a daily, weekly, or monthly basis?

Let's look again at the auto industry. Over the next decade, the auto industry will transform not only their product, but their method of transportation and delivery. From traditional auto manufacturers like Ford and GM to the innovators like Google, Apple, and Tesla, transformation will lead us into the future with products and services the general public is not even aware of today. As leaders create new systems, new industries will emerge, and new companies will experiment, such as Tesla Semi with its electric semi-trucks.

Deming's principles offer organizations anywhere in the world the strategic and operational foundation to transform themselves and their industries. His principles guide leaders to have the focus necessary to compete in our global economy. Though these principles were developed decades ago, they still remain relevant. In fact, these principles foreshadowed the evolution of business models and strategies that are constantly implemented today: the relentless integration of customer feedback into creating a more effective, innovative system; the evolution of the modern, information-based supply chain; and collaborative, interdependent connectivity within organizations that demands people work, learn, improve, and innovate together.

Deming's writings on teamwork, collaboration, rigorous training, and working closely with suppliers were among his most controversial and groundbreaking. He emphatically stated that the customer is the most important part of the production line, that fear inhibits cooperation and leads to the creation of false data, and that management by objectives (especially numerical goals and targets) creates organizational misalignment.

When leaders truly understand these principles, there is a huge opportunity for them, along with managers and employees, to make profound changes happen. Leaders using leadership theories based on systems thinking have fundamental insight into the changes in structure and strategy that organizations must make as they pursue the imperatives of innovation, speed, flexibility, quality, and creating value for customers and future markets.

Deming asserted that the greatest leverage for unleashing the potential for human performance in organizations, and thus for improving organizational performance, lies in rethinking the way we construct organizational reality. **The essential differentiator between survival and failure is a leader with profound knowledge and courage.** Many of the barriers to quality, improvement, and innovation are of our own making. Letting go of the assumptions that underlie prevailing business models is the key to removing these obstacles. This approach to rethinking the way we construct organizational reality raises organizational performance to new levels. We can, for example, improve and improve the buggy whip, but that improvement will never get us to a horseless carriage, an automobile, or an electric car. Only leaders who think about innovation, the future, and how to transform will help organizations survive.

—

Most business models that fail do not appreciate the degree of connectedness between elements of the organizations: between department silos, between customer-supplier relationships, between organizations and their customers, between the flow of process improvement and project teams, and between measurement systems and behavior. In too many organizations, there is a disconnect between the direction in which the leadership team is taking the organization and the project team's work. Each department works alone without understanding the aim of the larger whole or how the team or department fits into and contributes to that whole. Often, teams are unaware of the work being done by other teams. Poor leadership fails to guide the optimization of all the work or link it to the value it offers customers.

Individuals and teams can work hard and make their best effort, but the enterprise may still fail. Leadership is responsible for creating the system and optimizing it so that everyone is working together toward a common aim and transforming into a more effective system. All teams need to work interdependently toward that aim and the strategic goals of the organization.

CREATING A SYSTEM FOR OPTIMIZATION

Firstly, let's begin with some simple definitions that will inform much of what you'll read in this chapter.

DEFINITION OF A SYSTEM

A system is a network of parts or interactions that work TOGETHER for an aim or common purpose. (Examples include a car, body, school district, symphony, or sports team.) To illustrate, if all musicians in an orchestra play their best and loudest, then they will always make noise without cohesion. However, when the musicians are led by a conductor, they have a stronger understanding of their purpose. Some musicians will play loudly, others softly, and others, at times, not at all, to make beautiful music together. The success of a system is dependent on how well they are led and how well they work *together*. This leads us to define system optimization.

SYSTEM OPTIMIZATION

The leader's role is to optimize his or her system. What does that mean? To optimize the system, all of the parts must work together collaboratively and effectively to achieve the purpose of the system. As with the example of an orchestra, the goal is to create beautiful music. The conductor leads and directs the musicians to play, optimizing the whole system to achieve a seamless performance.

There is also a distinction which needs to be addressed here. Optimize is not the same as maximize. We may rarely hear the word optimize, but we do often hear that results have to be maximized. If the musicians maximized their playing, and each played their best and loudest individually, the performance would be noise. To reiterate, the leader's job is to optimize the system and lead it to be successful. The leader does that by guiding all to work toward the same aim and purpose. The leader is *accountable* for the system and guiding and communicating with the group to accomplish their work together. The players are responsible for contributing to the aim. The distinction between accountable and responsible is an essential one for leaders and is further explored in a later section.

TRANSFORMATION

Transformation is the creation and/or change of a whole new form, function, or structure. To transform is to create something new that has never existed before and could not have been predicted from the past. Transformation means that the new state cannot go back to the old state. The butterfly can't go back to a caterpillar. Likewise, when people transform their thinking and behaviors, they can't go back to the old way of thinking and behaving. A micromanager doesn't go back to micromanaging when he has discovered the devastating impact he had on his staff and how more effective he is when he leads, inspires, and develops people.

THE LEADER'S ROLE

Leaders must understand how systems and processes work together toward their aim. Their role is not only to create the system, but to optimize it. What does that mean? Optimization means making a system perform as well as it is capable of doing with all of its parts working together. The role of each part of a system is not to do its best independently. Rather, it is to contribute toward optimization of the system as a whole.

Think about your body—how well would it work if your parts were competing with each other? Would it function well or go into shock? Would the car career off the track and crash if it was built only to maximize toward a top speed? The difference between optimize and maximize is significant. Leaders and coaches must understand it and communicate the difference. A team working together to optimize will outperform most systems over time than a team that tries to maximize.

The greater the interdependence between parts, the greater the need for cooperation between them. It is the job of leadership to make sure the parts work together—and this job cannot be delegated!

THE IMPORTANCE OF SYSTEMS

Why is the system important? If leaders do not understand how to create a system, optimize it, transform it, and use it, the system will struggle, decline, and eventually fail. Some systems are huge, and their demise takes a long time. In the 1980s, when IBM was floundering, management guru and author of *Everyday Heroes*, Dr. Gluckman, keenly observed, "IBM is like a big dinosaur; it will just take longer to come to its knees." It is that way with any struggling major corporation or education system. And the tidal wave can wreak havoc throughout the industry.

If the systems around us are not well-led and continually transforming, they will fail. Economic systems, banking systems, school systems, health care systems, and political and corporate systems are all subject to failure. The systems we witness failing are those which do not transform.

Leaders can turn their system around, but where do they begin? It takes the leadership team's commitment to new learning, testing experiments, and new actions and behaviors to make a profound difference. What kind of executive or business owner calls for help? One who has tried everything he can think of and needs additional resources. Or one who needs guidance on issues with which she's not familiar and reaches out to someone else for assistance. The requests come in all shapes and sizes. But what is most important to remember is that a wise and knowledgeable leader is one who recognizes that he needs help and that he doesn't have all the answers or knowledge. The unsolved problems and issues that emerged ten or twenty years ago still exist today.

OPEN TO LEARNING

One day, as I was boarding a flight in New York, a colleague called and said, "I have a company that needs some strategy assistance. Can you help?" We agreed to chat the next morning, and I got some background about the business. Jim Leale, the business owner, called soon after that, and we set up a time to meet. The reality was that the company needed to transform to survive. Jim could either keep the same system that was not producing the results he needed or commit to going on a very tough journey to succeed. Fortunately, Jim was open to learning.

But there was a lot of history of poor communication and manipulation. Certain employees often asked for help or favors in their personal lives. Other people wouldn't talk to their colleagues. They wouldn't support each other in getting the work done if they wanted to show that they had control over someone else. The barriers to success were numerous. With the use of the Strategic Compass, I created a management team and began asking them new questions and teaching them new management principles. It was evident that not everyone in the company was interested in working together. There were supervisors who preferred to have power and control *over* other people. If that didn't work well, there would be internal battles and dysfunctional gossip, blaming, judging, and criticizing. There were those people who said, "Yes, great idea; I can make that improvement," and then would walk off and do the work the old way. The work, communication, and paperwork didn't flow. There were few efficient systems and processes, and the working environment needed a major change.

I recruited Operations Director Babette Shelton, and she joined the Leale's team and helped focus them on process improvement and relentless service to the customers. The Leale's team focused on improving the quality of everything: work flow, communication, information, supporting each other, and achieving great customer feedback. Waste, complexity, arrogant attitudes, bottlenecks, and barriers to improvement were dramatically reduced. New services and opportunities were pursued. People worked together and solved problems like never before. Revenues tripled.

Previously, Babette had been the youngest manager on a management team I formed and guided fifteen years ago (at the largest sales volume used car dealership in California). In this fast-paced, competitive industry where the owners hoped to grow their business from $30 to $40 million, the team abandoned their old thinking and behaviors, transformed, and took the company from $30 to $300 million in three years. When people learned that the problems emerge from the system that management has created, the owners and their team began to change the system. The focus became on improving the system, and the people stopped blaming, judging, and criticizing each other. The employee turnover rate went from 40 percent per month to virtually zero. The power of people working together brings results never before achieved—or imagined.

The most important value that most of the Leale's employees shared was their commitment to the customer's happiness and satisfaction. That was their foundation. That also meant that there were aspects of their commitment that could stand to improve, but it was a healthy place to start.

The team defined its compelling purpose and direction. It explored key methods, issues, and opportunities, and how those concepts interacted. They identified and prioritized resources. People began learning about improving their processes and communication skills. But some people, although highly skilled, didn't want to improve and didn't fit into the new system. They were given the opportunity to contribute to a new way of working; they could be "in" or "out." Some left.

Each time an unsatisfied employee left, there was more flow, collaboration, and trust, less fear, and better communication. New employees joined the team and were eager to contribute their ideas and work interdependently. It was a challenging task to create such vastly new systems and processes, and to develop better leadership, communication, and a healthier work environment, but the energy and self-motivation of the people made a difference.

The revenue in my client's company has tripled with about the same number of people. The industry usually has its slow months in the winter. But I challenged the team to change their thinking, challenge that belief, and adopt a new one in its place: there would be no slow season. By what method would the winter months be as robust as the other seasons? With their aim, the team created a system that delivered the highest revenue ever in the history of the company, in the "slow season." Every year, the revenues continue to trend up. Everything has improved and is continually on that path toward better quality. For this leadership team, optimizing their system and making sure they chose survival as their option made all the difference.

—

In *The Fifth Discipline: The Art & Practice of the Learning Organization*, author Peter Senge describes the automobile industry's awakening to systems thinking. When American automobile manufacturers began to take Japanese competition seriously, they dissected engines from their cars and from Japanese cars. They found that three subassemblies in the American car engine used three differently sized bolts. This necessitated three sets of tools, three sets of inventory, and so on. The Japanese car used the same-sized bolt throughout. The conclusion was that each American subassembly was intended to be independently effective. In the Japanese production system, someone was responsible for making sure that the entire assembly was interdependently effective.

All parts of an enterprise are connected: systems, subsystems, processes, projects, materials, resources, people, teams, products, and services. All contribute. But when the system doesn't deliver the results we want or need, what do we do? We blame people. However, only leadership is accountable for the success of systems, because leaders create the systems. Individuals are responsible for contributing their parts but cannot be held accountable for a system they did not create, nor can they be responsible for its outcomes, contrary to common practice in the

United States and other countries that have adopted West-ern-style management.

THE RELATIONSHIP BETWEEN SYSTEMS AND CUSTOMERS

Customers are also a part of the system, and we need their feed-back. Years ago, a Wisconsin state tax manager, Ralph, retired after thirty years in the department. His assistant, Betty, had worked with him for at least half of his career. The new manager, Scott, took the reins and began to observe how the department operated and how they supported the other departments. After a few months, Scott noticed that at the end of every month, Betty was at her desk beyond her normal hours, a bit short in her re-sponses, and that most people avoided her during the last days of the month. After a couple of anxious days spent deciding what to do, Scott approached Betty and asked her what she had been so diligently working on. She said, "The monthly report that goes to all of the department heads." He asked what it contained, and she proudly showed him her work. He asked what the depart-ment managers do with the report. She didn't know. But she showed him the hallway of bookcases where she neatly filed all of the reports in binders. He asked, "Does anyone ever comment or ask questions about the report?" She said, "Never." He asked, "Why do you do it?" She obediently answered, "Ralph said that we should compile and distribute the information in case anyone ever needed it." Amazed, Scott asked, "How long have you been doing this monthly report?" (He would later learn that it took her three days to compile and distribute it.) Betty responded, "Thir-teen years." There were bookcases with binders that held all of the reports for the *thirteen years*. But no one read them.

There are times when there is no customer involved in the work that we're doing, and other times when we don't know or understand the customers' needs. Understanding the purpose of our work and understanding the needs of our customers and how to best serve them can help focus and deliver the service they want. Extra efforts that are not required in the delivery of this service are waste and need to be eliminated.

It is important to remember that the optimization of a system does not result from the optimization of individual pieces. Marian Hirsch, a senior technical editor at a global bioscience company, had an opportunity to help her team save a project and optimize the system. She explained: "Last week I was in a department meeting to kick off a project that was a small part of introducing an updated version of a product (Product A). This introduction has important strategic implications for our business sector. We have a modernized format for manuals, and we are revising older ones to match this new format as products change.

"The writer assigned to this new project was assigned to update the format of a manual for a different product (Product B), the content of which wasn't scheduled to change for a while. The manager wanted to slap some minor changes in the manual for Product A. I introduced the group to the system and its interactions: the product life cycle, company strategy, impact on customers, etc. Together we discovered and learned that it was a better investment to completely update the manual for Product A; [the quality] would be better for customers, [and it would] have a longer life and make more sense for the investment of time and money. We could do the manual for Product B a few months down the road with no negative consequences. We just needed to look outside of our project as a team, look at the entire portfolio and marketing strategy, and understand how we fit in and were contributing toward it."

If top management focuses on creating an optimal system in which people can collaborate on projects, continually improve processes, and innovate, then transformation is possible. If a company works on transformation and strives to make a difference internally and in society, won't financial success be a natural result?

UNDERSTANDING VARIATION

Variation is normal. Numbers go up. Numbers go down. The trick is knowing how to manage variation (not just reduce it) and knowing when to act, not react or tamper with numbers. Knowing when to take action and when to be hands-off is important for the successful implementation of improvement initiatives. Otherwise, things that aren't broken get "fixed" (tampered with), and things that are broken are left unattended. Understanding variation is key to reading any measurement of a process and, in turn, understanding how to optimize the enterprise. If data are interpreted improperly, managers will be very likely to react inappropriately and make poor decisions.

STRATEGIC QUESTION FOR YOUR COMMITMENT

A few years ago, my colleagues and I were just beginning to teach a group of executives in a Silicon Valley high-technology corporation about improvement strategies. We observed the data from one department and noticed that it was "too perfect." There was little variation and few errors, yet the results the department was producing were abysmal. It didn't make sense. The only answer to this discrepancy was tampered data—numbers were being represented inaccurately on the charts to reflect better outcomes. Upon deeper investigation, we learned the vice president of the department was the culprit. Why would he do that?

When the senior leader commits to transforming the organization, he simultaneously begins to stir the "fear pot." There are hundreds of instances in which fear can emerge in an organization, particularly during times of change. Often people feel the fear but aren't able to identify or articulate it. When an organization begins to improve, change is inevitable. There are hundreds of kinds of fears, and they can impact anyone, at any level, with any title. The most common kinds of fear that come from change within an organization are fear of losing one's job or business, fear of change, of failure, of speaking up, of making mistakes, of the unknown and uncertainty, and of saying "no" or "I don't know."

My colleagues and I met with the president to share our discovery that the vice president had been manipulating the data. He was surprised about his VP's behavior. We assured the president that his VP's behavior was not uncommon. The VP was fearful because he did not know if he could learn and adapt to change, and therefore felt forced into manipulating the company data to make his department look more efficient. We all had a discussion with him. He admitted being afraid of the upcoming changes. What if he could not learn as fast as his colleagues or made mistakes? The president assured him that the purpose for collecting data was to understand a process and improve it, not to find people to blame for problems in the system. We assured him that the team would learn and work to improve together.

The VP was relieved, and his fears were reduced. He could focus on learning how to adapt and integrate new improvements, and subsequently contribute to the necessary work of the team. Both the president and vice president learned valuable lessons during the process. The president realized that he needed to better communicate to reduce the fear that could cause stress in his employees. The vice president learned that he had to explore in himself the fears that would come up in a changing environment. He had to ask questions of the president and work together with his colleagues to build more trust.

The senior leader must have courage to challenge his or her employees and to set high goals for the company. To make progress, hard decisions have to be made. Coaching and educating the leadership team is essential. Although everyone learns at a different rate and in different ways, the team has to move forward together. Just as the vice president and president had individual lessons to learn, their collaboration was also essential. It takes courage and trust on both ends. Oftentimes consultants see managers who are change-averse. If someone is continually a barrier to progress despite coaching and new learning, you, as a leader, must ask them the question, "Are you in, or are you out?" Either they are willing to adopt new principles (though they may be challenging), or they no longer fit within the organization.

There is variation in people's understanding of other people's behaviors. Likewise, there's variation in the tools that management seeks to use. Six Sigma has become a well-known management fad over the past couple of decades as a popular application for statistical process control. Organizations using it attempt to improve processes so that there are only 3.4 defects or mistakes per million. However, many managers do not really understand what Six Sigma is, nor do they understand its limitations—they focus only on its ability to reduce defects. They have rolled many dysfunctional practices into it, actually sub-optimizing their organizations in the process. There are better tools, such as run charts and control charts based in the theory of variation, that support quality process improvement, innovation, and system optimization. That said, Six Sigma should be used only as a tool and not a management method, because processes (and people) are not alike. Six Sigma is often improperly used because many users do not understand statistical thinking or the theory of variation.

Deming provides an example of theory of variation in which he performs his "red bead experiment." Deming shows that no matter the diligence of work performed by workers or even managers, no worker can control the number of red beads they scoop up. This experiment shows how natural variation will occur in any process, and we can look to the data to determine what variation looks like.

In Don Wheeler's book *Understanding Variation: The Key to Managing Chaos,* he writes, "Data are collected as a basis for action. Yet before anyone can use data as a basis for action the data have to be interpreted. The proper interpretation of data will require that the data be presented in context, and that the analysis technique used will filter out the noise."[4] For leaders to make wise decisions about their organizations, their time is better spent applying the theory of variation and making decisions based on looking at their critical data over time.

Understanding variation is key to reading any measurement of a process and, in turn, understanding how to optimize the enterprise. If data are interpreted improperly, managers will be very likely to react inappropriately and make poor decisions.

The graph of data (below) is from the human resource department for a major organization. The graph shows statistics for the amount of time the department takes to fill a critical hiring requisition. The data are useful to the company because they suggest uncontrolled conditions and show the average time it will take to fill hiring requisitions.

Analyzing the data by comparing a single point in one year over a single point in another year can lead to over-adjustments. For example, comparing statistics from May 2007 against those from December 2008 shows that the hiring time increased in 2008. While this is true, managers shouldn't extrapolate that minor variance to mean a significant, negative trend in hiring practices is occurring. Natural variances occur in any system; managers should look for long-term trends when deciding whether process-improvement initiatives are needed. The data point for January 2008, however, shows a clear outlier. Management should investigate what caused this divergence from the other data and

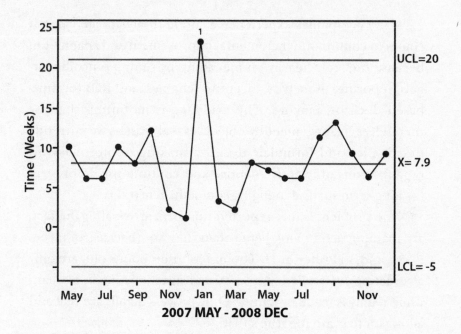

ensure that control mechanisms are in place to prevent it from happening again.

As I observed one statistician at an American defense manufacturer explain:

"Most management has no clue about variation. Project managers are forced to work with poorly designed tools and standard operating procedures that make things worse. Project management software cannot even deal with common-cause variation. It's useful for tracking progress, but completely useless for making predictions. Garbage in, garbage out—and people rely on it without asking any questions, much less pertinent ones! It doesn't tell you if the process is stable. One example is when one of my technical leads tried to trim our team's schedule to fit a more aggressive product launch—the software added six weeks to the project!"

There needs to be a continual pursuit of improvement. That's fundamental. In the book *Toyota Kata*, author

Mike Rother writes:

"Many companies experience a subtle disadvantage when it comes to continuous, incremental improvement and adaptation, because they rely heavily on managing by setting outcome targets, reporting of metrics, incentive schemes, and ROI formula-based decision making. The evidence is mounting that, by themselves, management by objectives—at least as we currently practice it—and formulaic decision making do not make an organization sufficiently adaptive and continuously improving for long-term survival in highly competitive markets.

"One problem is that reported numbers arrive after the fact, are manipulated to look better than they are (because of incentives), and, as Professor H. Thomas Johnson points out, are only abstractions of reality. Metrics are abstractions made by man, while reality is made by nature. Only process details are real and allow you to grasp the true situation."[5]

Variation, statistical thinking, and asking questions that don't allow for tampering are imperative concepts that all leaders must adopt.

SEEKING KNOWLEDGE

People managing systems and working in them need to collaborate to develop methods by which processes can be continually improved and results achieved. The most critical question that leaders must ask themselves when seeking improvement is, "What are we trying to accomplish together?" (Remember, the question "What are we trying to accomplish?" is not sufficient; adding the word "together" encourages people to look at a larger aim, not just their own part in it.) The next question should be, "By what method?" In other words, what strategies and processes will we use? Finally, people managing systems must ask, "What measures of improvement will we use so that we can identify a change and know if it is truly an improvement and significant enough to make a difference?"

While company leaders put an emphasis on numerical goals, objectives, and targets, that may not help them achieve their results. Simultaneously, it's important to discuss the plan and methods by which progress toward those goals might be achieved. Setting arbitrary numerical goals alone causes the first major crack in the system and its interactions and connections. The oft-repeated axiom, "If it can't be measured, then it can't be managed" is one of the most ludicrous beliefs about measurement. What are we thinking when we say this (or are we thinking?)? The more accurate axiom is, "If it can be measured, then it can be improved." But, if it can't be measured, can it also be improved? What if we endeavored to seek quality and knowledge rather than only numbers?

There are hundreds of examples that refute this nonsense, but here's a common sense one: Let's say we asked parents, "Do you feel it is important to play with your children?" Most people would agree that playing with children is very important; it encourages their creativity and learning and offers other benefits. What if we asked, "Do you measure the time you play with them?" Most parents would say, "No, why would I do that? I know it is important, and so I spend time with my child whenever possible." We might reply, "Then why not measure it?" After all, the common belief in organizations both large and small is that if it is truly important, it can and must be measured. But what would we measure: the number of minutes we play? The number of activities? The number of times the child asks a question about the rules of the game?

—

Metrics aren't always known, quantifiable, or meaningful, and not everything can or should be measured. Dr. Deming attributed this brilliant insight to Dr. Lloyd Nelson, director of statistical methods at Nashua Corporation: "The most important figures for management of any organization are unknown and unknowable." Measurement mania has thrown many of our systems into decline. Our education system, for example, focuses on measuring, testing, and rewarding teachers with merit pay rather than on building a system that encourages joy in learning and develops lifelong learners and responsible contributors to society. How do we measure the joy of a lifelong learner or the contributions one makes as a result of that joy of learning? The most important measurements are unknown.

The purpose of measurement is to help us determine whether we are going in the right direction to achieve our organization's strategic goals. For every decision we make, every project and process we work on, will our work, and the metrics we track, help us get closer to our aim, or further away?

Big data is a booming industry, and data scientists are emerging everywhere. What has caused this new obsession with data? It's easy to measure almost everything. Measuring everything provides some sense of comfort to many people who need to make decisions based on data. However, measuring and analyzing everything is a colossal waste of time, energy, and resources. It's often the case that when people become overloaded with data, they cannot make useful decisions. Big data is one of the latest management fads generated by large corporations.

While the push to measure *everything* is ludicrous, it is essential for executives and process improvement teams to use data in context to make wise decisions, observe trends, track sustainable flow, and make predictions.

—

It was one of my early visits to a new client company, and we had arranged to meet in the conference room. I got to the room first, and several minutes later, a couple of people began bringing in boxes filled with charts printed in four-color ink. I asked what all the boxes were, they said, "We thought you would want to see all of our work." Their printer must have been in overdrive! The meeting kicked off, and I began asking basic strategic questions: What are you trying to accomplish? By what method? How are you measuring the progress of your key processes? How are they interrelated? How are you serving your customer, and how do you know? How are you making your decisions? There were specific measures that reflected their work, as well as the process flow and outcomes, and their success with their customers. Their progress was trending in the right direction. The meeting was short. They could focus their conversations more on the *essential measures* and critical success factors and decide what needed to be improved that would make a difference to their customers. And they could stop spending days and days gathering every process data point. That quantity of the data gathered wasn't needed. The quality of the data gathered over time would be able to help the team understand the process better and help them to make pertinent decisions.

Measures are essential, but metrics mania is not. Data is not knowledge. Data can be gathered and used with information. It only becomes knowledge when you apply it.

Acquiring knowledge is a powerful asset in any organization. It helps improve and accelerate process improvements and decisions. As Ikujiro Nonaka and Hirotaka Takeuchi wrote in their book *The Knowledge-Creating Company,*

"Knowledge officers are responsible for justifying the value of knowledge that is constantly being developed by the crew. They need to decide strategically which efforts to support and develop. We have found that qualitative criteria, such as truthfulness, beauty, or goodness, are equally as important as quantitative criteria, such as efficiency, cost, or return on investment."[6]

Often, it can be useful to implement a tool first shared by Dr. Walter Shewhart at AT&T Bell Labs as the Plan Do Check Act model of continuous improvement. This tool was adopted and made popular by Dr. Deming as the Plan-Do-Study-Act (PDSA) model.

The first step of the PDSA model is to plan, yet some people are resistant to planning. They think planning is too time-consuming, and they prefer instead to jump into a project and start doing. Planning does not need to be a boring or lengthy process, but the more thorough the planning process, the more opportunities the team has to build out a process adequately. It's important to discuss what will be done and who will do what. Sometimes team members can even practice or rehearse. The more a team can plan, the more they can anticipate challenges and how to address them. Planning is a dynamic process, and anticipating and communicating throughout it can add a lot of collaboration and creativity.

For example, rare surgical procedures are an ideal opportunity for intense planning. Surgeons may have only one chance to have a successful outcome, such as separating conjoined twins. They have a well-trained team that will participate in many hours of planning about how they will separate the twins. They anticipate as much as they can so they will be prepared. Then they perform the surgery. After it is finished (successfully we hope), they debrief so they can capture lessons they can integrate and improve next time and discard what doesn't work.

Building five hundred tract homes requires a plan and some modifications during the building process, but it does not have the same level of intensity as a life and death scenario. A group of friends or family can plan a trip to Europe and either prepare a very structured trip or have a very loose agenda and adapt as they travel. A manufacturing plant has a new product line, and to

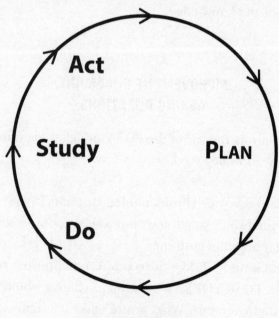

The PDSA Circle

assemble a product, they can run many PDSA cycles during the day to improve the quality and efficiency. The more frequently and faster the PDSA can be used, the more quickly the team can acquire more knowledge and make improvements. The PDSA is as powerful as the conversations, sharing, data gathering, idea flow, and implementation.

Using the PDSA faster not only helps you acquire more knowledge together but allows you to gain the competitive edge.

THE PDSA CYCLE OF CONTINUAL IMPROVEMENT (PLAN-DO-STUDY-ACT)

Dr. Deming also referred to the PDSA cycle as the Shewhart Cycle, named after Dr. Walter Shewhart, who taught the cycle of continuous improvement to Dr. Deming.

The PDSA cycle can be defined as the "dynamic scientific process of acquiring knowledge."

IMPROVEMENT PHASE ONE: ASKING QUESTIONS

Before beginning the use of the PDSA model, some fundamental questions need to be asked.

1. What bugs you? (Problem identification.) What is keeping you from doing your job better or faster? What bugs the customer?
2. What would WE like to accomplish to improve the work TOGETHER? What kind of change would be an improvement? What would make it a significant improvement?

3. What is repetitive—what is it that keeps happening over and over that is frustrating?
4. What can we measure?
5. What changes can you make that will result in improvement?

IMPROVEMENT PHASE TWO:
USING THE PDSA CYCLE, QUICKLY & REPETITIVELY

Assess the current situation.

PLAN: Plan a test or a change aimed at improvement.
DO: Carry it out (preferably on a small scale first).
STUDY: Study the results. Use data in context. What did we learn?
ACT: Adopt the change OR abandon the change OR run through the cycle again, possibly under different conditions.

"Experience teaches us (enables us to plan and predict) only when we use it to modify and understand theory." Dr. Deming

Questions to address when using the PDSA cycle:

PLAN:
What process needs improvement?
Why choose this process to improve?
What do our customers tell us about this process? What adds value for them? What adds no value?
What changes are desirable?
What data are available? (Mistakes, defects, rework, waste, cycle time, is the process in control?)

Who should be on the team?

What would be the most important accomplishment of this team?

Are new observations needed?

Are tests necessary?

Do we all understand the process?

What are the possible outcomes?

What are our options?

Which option is most promising in terms of new knowledge or profit?

How will we create an environment for learning?

Why is the problem occurring? (ask why five times)

How will we measure success and progress?

What possible obstacles may we face as we work to improve this process?

What will we do to overcome the barriers to improvement?

DO:

What data do we have?

What tools do we need to use to discover more data?

How will we collect and analyze the data?

What is the plan to implement?

Will it be implemented first on a small scale?

How will it be introduced on a larger scale?

How will the results be captured and analyzed?

STUDY (focus on building knowledge):

What did we learn?

Do our results correspond to our expectations?

What went wrong?

Did you work according to the plan?

What are the critical success indicators or key quality characteristics?

How are they being monitored?

What needs to be improved?

ACT:

Shall we standardize?

What do we need to do to standardize?

Shall we do another PDSA?

Does this standardization make a difference to the customer?

Who needs communication about the new process?

Who needs training?

What data are you gathering from customers?

What are the next steps?

Use the PDSA model to: (1) create a dialogue for brainstorming, information sharing, exploring options to problem solving, or looking at new opportunities; (2) gather knowledge quickly; (3) facilitate change rapidly; to better create or understand the system and move it in the direction you need it to go.

START

UNDERSTANDING PEOPLE

MOTIVATORS

Here is a list of extrinsic motivators (which come from outside forces, such as rewards and money) and intrinsic motivators (which come from the inside, such as pride in work and a desire to serve others). Which most motivate you?

Societal Insight
Higher Service
Mastery, Knowledge
Influence
Collaboration
Curiosity/Search for Opportunities
Aggression
Anger
Desire
Fear
Tension
Indifference
Guilt/Shame/Blame

In addition to extrinsic and intrinsic motivators, the following questions also help us reflect about what motivates us, what results we achieve, and whether these results are satisfying:

Who are we? What motivators drive us?
How do motivators inform our behavior and strategies?

What results do we get?

Where would we like to be?

What motivators do we need to get there?

How can the shift happen?

What are the changes we need to make and results we wish
to reap?

In his book *Intrinsic Motivation at Work,* Kenneth Thomas explains the importance of allowing employees to make their own decisions. He writes, "Choice takes on extra importance when we are committed to a meaningful purpose. Then a sense of choice means being able to do what makes sense to you to accomplish the purpose."[7] Consider how the reflection questions and Thomas's quote are related. How much pride can employees take in work that they aren't motivated to complete?

Results—such as financial results, sales quotas, and customer satisfaction—and variation in results are informed by the environment, processes, equipment, material, and people. Most of the time, we attribute all results (and variation) to people, particularly the people who are closest to the results.

For example, we tip a waitress less because the food was improperly prepared (variation in the process), or the service was slow (variation in the environment, because two other waitresses called in sick). A project manager, whose results are compared to budgets, quota, or goals, is considered successful or unsuccessful based on how well the negotiations went during last year's budgeting meeting. Salespeople hold or accelerate sales or sales returns, thus distorting figures, to meet goals and quotas. If a sales rep meets his or her quota for the period five days early, he or she might hold new sales orders until the next period begins to help ensure that he or she will meet the next period's quota.

Daniel Pink, author of *Drive: The Surprising Truth about What*

Motivates Us, offers a new perspective on what drives our motivation. He writes, "So we have a choice. We can cling to a view of human motivation that is grounded more in old habits than in modern science. Or we can listen to the research, drag our business and personal practices into the twenty-first century, and craft a new operating system to help ourselves, our companies, and our world work a little better."[8]

The role of leaders is *not* to motivate workers. Top management is responsible for creating the environment where people feel *self-motivated*. Employees should feel motivated to do excellent work so that they can contribute to serve their customers. Employees and project teams work *in* the system. While they are responsible for their own behavior, they cannot be held accountable for the results of the system with its many interdependent parts that often fail to connect.

If an organization and the project teams within it succeed, it is because top management has made a significant commitment to transform the company into a thriving, dynamic, developing, learning organization with a management philosophy grounded in theories, not management fads.

TRANSFORMING, NOT MERELY CHANGING

Ask yourself, are you committed to deep learning? Are you prepared to question your beliefs, assumptions, and practices? If you have been successful, can you really challenge yourself? Can you lead and inspire people like never before?

Can you *transform*?

OPERATIONAL DEFINITION

To transform means to change in form, appearance, or structure, or to create something new that has never existed before and perhaps could not have been anticipated. Organizational transformation happens when leaders develop a vision of transformation and a system for continually questioning and challenging beliefs, assumptions, patterns, habits, and paradigms. Leaders who understand this will ask challenging, cutting-edge questions. They use valuable tools for accomplishing transformation that have already been laid out throughout this book, including the Strategic Compass and system diagrams. Additionally, if leaders strive to continually apply management theory through the lens of systems and statistical thinking, they will be well on their way toward truly transforming.

One CEO from the Midwest explains it well:

"Becoming a transformational leader is not easy. It's hard to stop doing what you've always done; ask the tough questions; challenge the status quo; admit that you don't know the answers;

and focus on delivering value the customer wants while sustaining the organization."

Organizational transformation occurs first in individuals, then in the organization itself. It requires a change in mindset. It requires leaders to understand systems thinking, statistical thinking and variation, prediction, and the psychology of people and culture. It also demands that leaders take decisive action. Transformation means leading an organization into the unknown, and that is often uncomfortable for many leaders. Leadership takes courage. This is why communication, collaboration, rapid learning, and working together toward the unified aim of the organization are fundamental.

Transformation is the real key to a business's survival and leadership position. An organization that is unable to achieve its potential must transform, which means that first, its leaders must personally transform themselves. To change the organization and to achieve better results, leaders need to think, do, question, and feel differently, not just measure differently. They must challenge their current beliefs, assumptions, and practices.

If leaders succeed in transforming their thinking and actions, their companies may survive, even innovate. If they do not, their organizations decline, and failure is imminent—no matter how hard people work, how brilliant their new ideas are, how efficiently processes flow, or how well project teams collaborate. Some will struggle and fail within months, while others may take years or even decades. For example, there are on average 6,000 startup companies in the Silicon Valley Bay Area in California at any time. On average, 90 percent of them will fail. When a Fortune 100 corporation is failing, people on the outside can usually see the decline long before the board or executives—the internal stakeholders—want to believe they're in trouble. But the truly great leaders are not in denial. They see the future, and they know they won't be part of it unless they transform their thinking and their organization.

Unfortunately, few individuals understand transformation or why it is an imperative. They don't understand why incremental or transitional change is not enough. People often confuse transformation with any kind of change, such as change management initiatives, technology breakthroughs, innovation, process improvements, or transitions. The truth is that all transformation is change, but not all change is transformation.

DISCERNING BETWEEN THE THREE DIFFERENT KINDS OF CHANGE

Many people assume that the "change" in "change management" refers to any kind of change. But leaders understand that change management is another fad and is not what they need to lead their organization into the future. Few changes are transformational. But transformational change is exactly the kind of change leaders need to focus on. Leaders see beyond the near future—they often see ten, twenty, or fifty years into the future. They investigate trends in their own industry and in society.

Executives who use either traditional or transitional kinds of change may not survive. Survival is optional. Leaders do not have to transform. But if they need to transform and innovate and do not, their organization will struggle, decline, and fail. There are many examples of corporations that have failed. The executives stayed on the sinking ship all the way down, oftentimes in denial that failure could ever happen to their company. They'd always been a success, so why did things all of a sudden stop working?

For example, Kodak was founded in 1888 in Rochester, New York and held the dominant position for decades in the photographic film industry. When the business began to decline in the late 1990s, their leaders were slow to transform and move into digital photography. They struggled to turn around and resisted innovation. Finally, in 2012, they filed for bankruptcy and sold many of their patents for $525,000,000 to corporations moving into the future (Apple, Google, Facebook, Amazon, Samsung, and others). Kodak as it was known did not transform and emerged after bankruptcy into a smaller and different business now owned by the UK-based Kodak Pension Plan.

But there are other executives who create or anticipate a new future and are open to or are actively driving disruption and innovation. They envisioned serving customers in new ways, creating new markets, and developing their people to invent new products and services that don't exist today. Hundreds of well-known founders have had a passion to build not just a widget, but a future. Whether it was Henry Ford, Tom Watson, Hewlett and Packard, Steve Jobs, Oprah Winfrey, or Jeff Bezos, at various times in their careers and corporations, these visionary executives have used all three types of change. Many executives use two types of change (transactional and transitional), and they may only need those. But to survive, a leader will have to transform through many disruptions (either in response to those the industry created, or with regard to disruptions they incited themselves in order to be able to move into the future with their ideas).

Change is a predictable part of life. We can shun it or embrace it. Each kind of change requires understanding:

- Various definitions
- Different kinds of thinking
- Strategies and methods
- Diverse results; different behaviors and various levels of outcomes; and
- Different kinds of changes in various areas/positions in an organization

ANOTHER VIEW: TRADITION, TRANSITION, TRANSFORMATION

So what does it take to change in various ways? Simply stated, we have a choice. If we as leaders want to hold on to our tradition, we will make incremental process improvements and not "rock the boat." In this mode, we may experience workers being content, complacent, arrogant, or unaware. If the world is changing in any significant way, it's only a matter of time before we have to change, too. The timing depends on the political environment, changes in the agency mission, and/or "The Washington Post Test," otherwise known as public opinion. We don't know if we'll have three months, three years, or thirty years, but it will eventually become clear that change is required.

If we want to move to the next level of change, yet remain safe, we must make linear step-by-step transitions and change from state A to state B. We know where we are going, and there is comfort in certainty. Many managers are willing to engage in what's normally been done without major changes. In transition, we can plan the change and work the plan. We can identify problems, create project or expert "tiger teams" of specialists in a particular field, and generate solutions.

But what if we want to create revolutionary change, build new systems and networks from the core, and capture new opportunities for the future? What if we let go and reach for the unknown? What if we anticipate a different future? We need transformation. We adopt the different and challenging strategies because we must. There are no road maps, milestones, Management By Objectives (MBOs), analytic cause-and-effect thinking, focus on individual performance, incentives, and quotas. It all begins with a new way of thinking and a deep commitment to learning, experimenting, discovering, and designing new value for customers (think Apple or Google or Space X). It means working in systems that don't create barriers for the employees who are yearning to do great work. The following are the three types of change, which are vital for any leader to be able to differentiate, especially when considering innovation within an organization—or outside.

TRADITIONAL CHANGE

Traditional change is necessary and helpful. Everyone in an organization can work together to improve communication, information sharing, the work processes, productivity, and to reduce waste and complexity. Improvement ideas can come from anywhere in an organization and be led at any level in an organization: from individuals who have a work process within their control, to project and cross-functional teams. The value of traditional change is that when tens of thousands of people in a bureaucracy are focused on improvements and striving toward greater quality, transformation (another type of change) has a foundation for success. Managers and workers across the organization can make daily contributions that culminate in greater improvements for customers or citizens. Traditional change is important and has the potential to engage many people in a bureaucracy or enterprise. But while traditional change has its place, it is also limiting because it does not ensure that an organization will optimally perform or survive.

TRANSITIONAL CHANGE

Transitional change is primarily concerned with problem-solving thinking (most prevalent throughout organizations, yet unsustainable; problems often reoccur because the processes are not improved). In transitional change, changes are made from one known process to another known process by planning a change and implementing it. For example, we can plan our annual vacation to our timeshare from one year to the next. Again, transitional change is helpful but limiting. As with traditional change, transitional change can be implemented anywhere in an organization.

The caution that people must take with transitional change is that too often problem-solving shifts to reactive firefighting. Instead of identifying problems, the symptoms of a problem are identified, and people work to stamp out the symptoms. The power of transitional change happens when symptoms are identified, the root causes of the problems are identified, and then, most importantly, the processes are improved (at the level where the symptoms and problems were emanating) with both a short-term and long-term focus. The fire is put out, the cause of the fire is determined, and the process is improved so that there is not another fire next week. This type of short-term thinking and problem assessment is the furthest from sustainable.

Project management is a form of transitional change. People work together to accomplish tasks and complete projects that will meet a need for the citizens or customers. *"The work is done; move on to the next problem,"* is often the mindset. The challenge in transitional change is that the improvements can be limiting. Transitional change includes much of the "best practice" and benchmarking thinking we discussed earlier. Managers and teams are willing to adopt new ideas when they are given the step-by-step manual that makes sense to them, and they can see how it's been of value to another department or workplace. However, by the time best practices have been identified, it can be argued that the company is already too late, and three steps behind the real innovators who aren't looking for road maps. Even if leaders maintain a continual process improvement mindset, their thinking and actions do not ensure that the organization markedly improves performance and services for the citizens.

TRANSFORMATIONAL CHANGE

Transformation is a change in "mindset," thinking, and actions. It means to change in form, appearance, or structure. Transformation in the context of the management of organizations and systems occurs first in individuals, and then in the organization. Transformation requires that leadership owns the transformation and is accountable for it. Transformation cannot be delegated.

Leaders work on transformation when they create and design and work ON the system. Staff and managers work IN the system. While people are responsible for their part in its improvement, only leadership is accountable for the transformation. Leaders must transform their own thinking continually and then create the communication that inspires their organization to transform with them. Transformational, cutting-edge thinking is imperative for an organization to thrive, innovate, and continually envision better futures.

The operational definition for transformation is as follows: Transformation is the creation and change of a whole new mindset, form, function or structure. To transform is to create something new that has never existed before and could not be predicted from the past. It is based on learning a system of profound knowledge, taking actions based on leading with new knowledge and courage, and communicating through effective diffusion strategy.

THREE TYPES OF CHANGES			
	Traditional	Transitional	Transformational
Motivation for Change	Better, Faster, Cheaper	Fix a problem	Survival, Environment, World Changes, Breakthrough needed
Degree of Change	Incremental improvements	Transition from old to new; A to B	Revolutionary, Necessary
Thinking	Improve	Change management; strategic planning	Radical shifts in mindset/thinking/ actions

Table continues

	Traditional	Transitional	Transformational
Actions	Manage and control processes	Design the plan; implement the plan	Whole system change, complete overhaul of mindset, paradigms, culture, communications, strategy, structure, actions, systems and processes, use of data, System of Profound Knowledge, cycles of Plan Do Study Act (PDSA)
Destination	Improvements; can be limited to improving the wrong things	Projects completed	Continually transforming; no end state
Change Requires	Improvement of skills, practices and performance; often limited to focusing on individual performance rather than the whole system to make significant differences	Controlled process/project managed/assigned	Senior leadership committed to new thinking, learning and actions; coaching from outside: "a system cannot see itself." Courage
Outcomes	Improvements, limited	Changes, limited	Sustainable change (with leadership and continual learning and new actions), new system: agile, adaptable, flexible, intelligent, emerging, connected, involved, creative, moving forward; ability to sense and respond

PART THREE

Where Do We Begin
to Transform?

Adapt THINK
Anticipate TRUST
Curious Intuitive Inclusive
Visionary Courage
Radical Fearless Plan Create
Do Future Implement
Coach Innovate Different Bold
Ideas Improve
New Daring
Flexible TRANSFORM
Customers
CREATE Dream

■ INTRODUCTION ■

In **Parts One** and Two, you learned what you need to STOP (and why), and how to START thinking differently by adopting new leadership thinking that will lead to better behaviors, actions, and results.

You are now able to ask those important questions that will lead to new answers and a better, bolder future. You are now able to more quickly identify barriers to improvement, and you know that you must pivot and shift your thinking before you can truly transform.

In Part Three, I discuss the final, essential component of leadership transformation: how to apply it. I share how by using a Strategic Compass, the System of Profound Knowledge, Communication Diffusion, a System of Transformation, and other interdependent theories, concepts, and tools, you can transform as a leader and achieve what you never dreamed was possible.

WHERE WILL YOU BEGIN YOUR JOURNEY?

Before you can begin transforming, you must understand where you are *now*. By taking the short assessment below, you will better grasp how ready you are to move forward in your own journey toward transformation. Your score on the first part will guide you on what you need to work on to improve your leadership thinking and actions. And your answers to the second part will provide you with some thoughts for reflection, and some opportunities to plan what you can do next.

How much work do you need to do? How can you challenge your thinking to improve your own beliefs, actions, and behaviors? How will you disrupt your own leadership? What are the stories that will create your legacy?

Survival Leadership Self-Assessment

Rate yourself on a scale from 1 to 10 with 1 being low and 10 being high in each category.

SCORE:

___ Courage

___ Commitment to Learning

___ Listening to Peers

___ Making Timely Decisions

___ Listening to Staff

___ Commitment to Learning with Others

___ Listening to Customers

___ Planning

___ Time Spent Discussing the Tough Issues With a Variety of People

___ Creating a Strategic Vision

___ Time Spent Communicating a Strategic Vision to All

___ Making Decisions Based on Data in Context

___ Ability to Apologize for Making Mistakes

___ Reading/Studying

___ Being Creative and Encouraging Creativity

___ Analytical Ability

___ Getting the Job Done

___ Reflecting

___ Understanding/Scanning the Larger Landscape
You Work In and Are Part Of

___ Understand Variation and Its Impact on Decision Making

___ Focus on Improving Your Own Leadership

___ Quality of the Time You Spend with Your Coach

___ Thinking About How All the Parts of Your System Work
Together to Achieve Its Purpose and Get the Results You
Want

___ Time You Spend to Appreciate People

___ Time You Spend to Plan for the Future

___ Time You Spend to Develop All People as Leaders

Add your score. **Total points:** _____

BASIC SCORES:

PERFECT SCORE: 260

200–260   A natural leader committed to learning, listening, and leading—and improving all of it. Dedicated to transformation and moving to new
levels. Will leave a positive legacy.

140–200   Potential for greater leadership. Need to identify
the barriers and limitations you may not see. Use
a coach or friend with systems knowledge to help
optimize (not maximize) your thinking and interactions.

80–140   Need to commit more time to develop leadership. Find someone with systems and transformation knowledge to help you think differently and reflect. Commit a large amount of time to question current beliefs and assumptions. Ask more questions about everything; assume you have few answers, and don't follow the "way we've been doing things," the status quo.

Under 80   Need drastic personal transformation for leadership. Probably display management practices that are control-oriented, demotivate people and create fear, waste, and lower productivity. Search for a guide to will ask you tough questions and push you to the edge of your comfort zone, yet encourage you to always be successful.

—

This next assessment will allow you to reflect on how your leadership connects with your organization.

Take this assessment now and then again two years from now and note the difference in your thinking. You should experience significant personal development and transformation in the interim.

Assessment Of Your Leadership Within Your Organization

1. What percentage of your week should you spend in strategic conversations about your business/work?

    (a) 5% (b) 20% (c) 50% (d) 75% (e) 90% (f) 100%

2. How many hours do you spend in strategic thinking and conversations per week?

    ___

3. Do you believe that internal competition will motivate employees?

    ❏ Yes ❏ No

4. Do you believe that you can motivate your employees in a healthy way?

    ❏ Yes ❏ No

5. The role of a leader is to create an environment where the fullest potential for human performance is unleashed, and people are self-motivated.

    ❏ True ❏ False

6. Instilling judgment, blame, and fear are the greatest demotivators of people.

    ❏ True ❏ False

7. Do you hold individuals accountable for the work and
    results?

    ❑ Yes   ❑ No

8. What percentage of your week do you spend listening
    to your employees?

    _____

9. What percentage of your week do you spend listening
    to your stakeholders?

    _____

10. How many times per day do you engage in
    conversations to communicate and help clarify
    your strategic purpose and how people fit into
    accomplishing it? Circle one.

    (a)Not daily (b)1 to 5 (c)5 to 20 (d)20 to 50 (e)50 to 100
    (f)More than 100

11. How many of your decisions are based on data
    gathered over time? Circle one.

    (a)None (b)A few (c)Most (d)All

12. Performance reviews are the preferred way to give
    employees feedback.

    ❑ True   ❑ False

13. Our system would perform better if our people would
    perform better.

    ❑ True   ❑ False

14. Our employees feel free to give honest feedback.

    ❑ True   ❑ False

15. What percentage of your employees knows the company's mission/purpose?

_____

16. Incentives are vital to a compensation system.

❑ True ❑ False

17. Individuals should be held accountable for achieving measurable goals.

❑ True ❑ False

18. Sound personnel policies are needed to control the workforce.

❑ True ❑ False

19. What percentage do employees participate in decision making?

_____

20. Profit is the most important measure of success.

❑ True ❑ False

21. Any decision that increases profits is a good one.

❑ True ❑ False

22. What percentage of your leaders/staff attend conferences/continuing education/seminars?

_____

23. Top performers should participate in an exclusive leadership development program.

❑ True ❑ False

24. How many hours per year do your managers and
executives spend on performance appraisals?

_____

25. What percentage of your time do you feel on the edge
of your comfort zone, learning and trying new things?

_____

26. How many times a day do people ask you questions
that challenge your current thinking, beliefs, or
practices?

_____

27. How do you react to questions and ideas that are out
of the norm and do not fit in the current culture?

_____

CREATE A SYSTEM FOR TRANSFORMATION

Leaders see their organization as a system. A leader understands that all of the parts of the organization are interconnected, and they only work if they work together. A leader recognizes that an organization is part of a larger system—an industry and society—and that system is one that the leader must create, build, improve, lead, and transform. The leader's job is to optimize the system, not to suboptimize it or maximize it.

The leader who is leading a system communicates a vision, a compelling purpose, the direction of the organization, its meaning (to internal and external customers), and its area of strategic focus that links to operational quality performance.

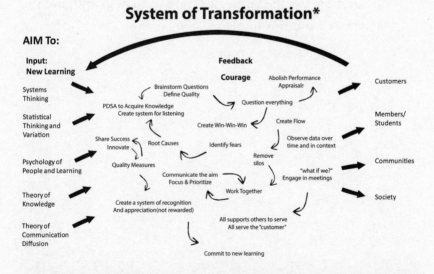

System of Transformation*

* Transformation defined: a mindset change resulting in new results and behavior

Following the assessment and your self-reflection, we now look at the elements we need to identify to create a system of transformation diagram. The System of Transformation is a nonexclusive illustration of some of the elements and interdependent parts necessary to transform. Here is an example of one that I created: To understand the System of Transformation in more detail, refer to the following applications:

- New learning on the left side of the diagram must happen to achieve transformation;
- The aim (compelling purpose—what and why are you choosing this aim) first must be defined;
- See that there are many elements working together to both remove barriers and optimize and accomplish the aim;
- Identify the various customers and define what they need from their perspective, and how they measure quality (of service or product);
- Create a robust, engaging system to ensure feedback is gathered, understood, and used;
- In addition, use the Strategic Compass to help optimize the system and transform.

THE PIVOTAL, POWERFUL STRATEGIC COMPASS

The Strategic Compass is a model that guides leadership thinking and helps leaders develop a cohesive business strategy. Leaders don't use road maps to grow and scale. Road maps are only useful when you know you are going from point A to point B.

Leaders use the Strategic Compass to guide their journey into the future and into new and unknown territory. It can help lead-

STRATEGIC COMPASS

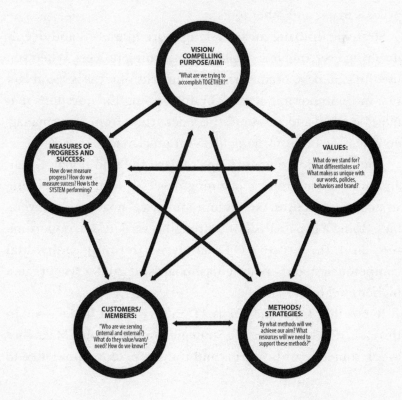

VISION/
COMPELLING
PURPOSE/AIM:
"What are we trying to accomplish TOGETHER?"

MEASURES OF
PROGRESS AND
SUCCESS:
How do we measure progress? How do we measure success? How is the SYSTEM performing?

VALUES:
What do we stand for? What differentiates us? What makes us unique with our words, policies, behaviors and brand?

CUSTOMERS/
MEMBERS:
"Who are we serving (internal and external?) What do they value/want/need? How do we know?"

METHODS/
STRATEGIES:
"By what methods will we achieve our aim? What resources will we need to support these methods?"

ers determine where they want to go and allow them to adapt along the way. It encourages them to look closely at the terrain, the barriers, and the opportunities (current customers and markets, potential partners, and potential markets) and make necessary shifts in response. Guided by this Compass, leaders can adjust, adapt, and be agile, responsive, and flexible in serving their customers. All of the five parts of the Strategic Compass are interactive and interdependent on the other parts, and all are needed to truly transform.

USING THE STRATEGIC COMPASS FOR SYSTEMS THINKING

The Strategic Compass has five foundational and interdependent parts. It is an essential tool for leadership, and it is often helpful for project teams (though project teams may also use road maps, process maps, and other tools).

Strategic thinking means asking more questions and deeply involving everyone in a challenging learning process. When you use the Compass, brainstorming hundreds of ideas is secondary to a more important activity: brainstorming the questions that must be asked and answered (it's a departure from many managers' focus on brainstorming ideas for quick fixes).

The Strategic Compass helps replace the traditional, linear, and often static strategic planning process that includes setting strategies, objectives, targets and numerical goals, and deliverables; doing a gap analysis or a strengths, weaknesses, opportunities, and threats (SWOT) analysis; defining individual competencies; and creating dashboards. It guides leaders to a higher level of thinking.

But as they say at the circus, "Don't try this at home"—or, in this case, don't complete the Strategic Compass alone. Make sure to ask someone with systems and transformation knowledge to facilitate your discussion, ask the challenging and unexpected questions, and ensure that you do not fall into groupthink. You will undoubtedly experience profound ah-ha moments and insights.

With the Strategic Compass you will achieve different (and better!) results. Oftentimes groups are so busy patting themselves on the back for their successes that they don't focus on strategy for the future, and they don't see the grenade that a competitor is throwing right at them.

COMMUNICATION DIFFUSION

Communication diffusion is essential for the application and implementation of transformation. It is necessary for effective use of the Strategic Compass and is the foundation on which all leadership principles are built.

Effective communication is important but very challenging for most. When more than five hundred senior executives across all sectors (corporate, nonprofit, military, health care, education, etc.) were asked about their biggest issue, and 99 percent reported that their number one challenge was communication.

Leadership needs to communicate effectively in multiple styles to connect with the many leading styles in an organization. A common assumption is that when the leader communicates the organization's aim and strategies, employees understand what it means and how they will contribute to the goal. This is immediately where communication begins to break down. Assumptions must be continually challenged.

It is the leader's responsibility to ask questions and to create an environment where leaders guide and explore ideas from all staff. Leaders should interact at much more frequent and varied levels via email, Skype, webinars, town hall meetings, open space technology, and by using guides like the Strategic Compass and the System Diagram that generate discussions that help people pursue their compelling purpose. They can also use statistical tools such as deployment flow charts, Pareto charts, and cause-and-effect diagrams to generate discussion about better data-driven decision making.

Leaders also must become more visible. They need to participate in more meetings with the goal of reiterating the company's aim and of asking questions about the strategies necessary to achieve goals and solve problems. In my client companies where leaders led their transformations, the executives were the first to participate in a multi-day strategic learning session that explored new leadership thinking. They often kick off subsequent sessions for managers, supervisors, and employees, and some executives even attend all or part of the learning sessions to deepen their own learning and hear the ideas that emerge from the robust and interactive discussions. With a new mindset and a deeper understanding of the kind of role needed to transform their organization, the leader spends more time engaging with the people and asking them, "How is your job going? What barriers do you face doing it better or faster? What other resources do you need? How can I help?" With their role as a student always seeking to learn and understand, the leader can better see and create a system that they can optimize.

The leader's level of engagement and asking questions of their vendors (see inputs on the System for Transformation Diagram) is also a part of their elevated intention to partner, work together, and find the win-win approach that will serve the customers. The leader's mindset shifts from being an adversarial judge and critic with a "my way or the highway" approach and win-lose thinking to one of "how do we work together to achieve a great product?" It becomes now a win-win-win-win strategy: wins for you, me, the System, and the customers.

A transformative leader also spends an increased amount of time engaging with customers. This is paramount, and it should go far beyond standard customer surveys. Leaders go visit customers to see how they are using their products and services. They ask questions about the customers' problems so that they can share that information and feedback with their organization.

This is the opportunity for process improvement teams to work together to provide better products and for innovators to create new and different products or services to offer current customers and potentially new markets.

With a more dynamic and robust communication system, the leaders can raise their level of engagement, learning, and understanding to continually transform their organization.

STRATEGIES FOR QUALITY AND GROWTH

Adopting **foundational strategies** will help disrupt current thinking, pivot the organization, and support a transformation. Three of the most important foundational strategies are:

- Quality: Every meeting and leadership initiative should start with a discussion that links what you're doing to serving the "customer," in whatever sector you're in.
- Continual Improvement: Every process, policy, and procedure should be questioned; how can it be improved? Link this strategy with the "customer" by asking how the improvement serves them.
- Innovation: How can we address future needs of "customers" and create markets for the future health of our organization and for society? How can we be bold and revolutionary?

If we want to capture a market, survive, and/or innovate, the above strategies are essential. As one of my clients always said, "It's not that hard!" But it is, especially at first. Why? Because our currents beliefs, assumptions, "best practices," and fads are barriers to success. First we need to shift our own individual thinking (personal transformation), and then get rid of these barriers to a better future.

Dr. Deming created a chain reaction toward quality, and the following illustration represents my interpretation of that thinking and how I guide its application:

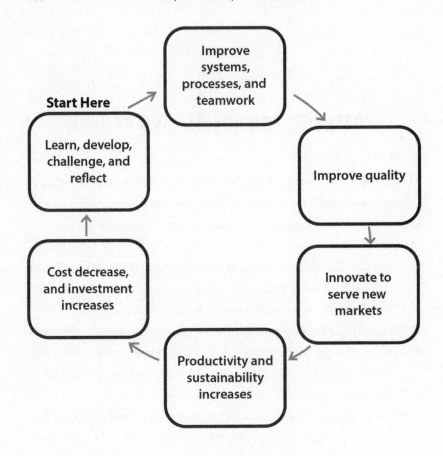

CAUTION: COST CUTTING IS NOT GROWTH

Some executives decide to cut costs as a method of growing their enterprise. Too often this action breaks down the organization and employees' morale, rather than fixing the organization's problems and improving the work and results. For example, the CEO of a Fortune 100 organization I worked with decided he would personally select a project to cut $10 million in expenses. He gathered a small team and set them off to work. In a few short months, they proudly accomplished their goal and were eager to share their results with the CEO. He thanked the team for their improvement ideas and encouraged them to implement them.

The problem here is that no one evaluated the potential negative impact of the cost-cutting methods. Across the organization, the team removed basic resources the employees needed to do their work. Office supply cabinets were empty, so people started bringing in supplies from home. The IT repair department's hours and resources were slashed, so if an employee's computer needed to be fixed or if their software had a glitch, that employee had to schedule a time with IT three days out, and then take their computer to another office to have it diagnosed. In the kitchenette, there was no coffee or tea. They did leave the water, but there were no cups! If an employee had a customer visiting and they asked for water, they told them that the CEO took the cups away.

After a few months, employees were exasperated and didn't want to struggle to get their (old, heavy) computers fixed and their work done. If their PowerPoint deck didn't get finished on time because their computer was down, they received both a scolding from their team leader (who might be in another state or country) and the threat of being put on a Performance Improvement Plan (PIP).

In those short months, turnover skyrocketed. People left and shared the stories of the "penny wise, pound foolish" thinking. The reputation of the company, corporate reviews on Glassdoor, and the stock price also plummeted. Employees found jobs where they were appreciated. The CEO suboptimized his system, the one that he was accountable for optimizing.

While costs can be managed, no corporation has ever grown their company by absurd cost cutting. Instead of doing this to your own organization, refer to the Strategic Compass for a new lens that enables you to ask bold questions whose answers are interdependent—it is then that you will be able to move your enterprise forward.

A CHILD'S LENS AND NEW LEARNING

Children see the world through a different lens. They cut through all of the complexity adults build up over the years. Their direct, innocent questions help people focus and do the right things.

If we can begin to view the world through that same child's lens—a lens of new knowledge—we will experience profound learning. Our application of new concepts and tools will be the catalyst for continual improvement, innovation, and effective communication. This commitment is often one that requires a leap of faith and begins at the top of any organization—military, corporation, school system, nonprofit, church, club, team, or government agency. The commitment is based in systems and statistical thinking, understanding people and their motivation, and diffusion of communication. These all contribute to the following process.

THE TRANSFORMATION AND LEARNING PROCESS

The Transformation and Learning Process requires that you:

1. Know that innovation in thinking and leadership is necessary to achieve a vision and that it will have an impact consistent with what you believe.
2. Ask provocative, strategic questions and challenge your current thinking and practices: Why are you

passionate about your career choice? What are you trying to accomplish to serve your customers/students/members? What is compelling you to work together to make a difference? What future do you want to create? What impact can you have on society?

3. Commit to learning and putting in practice new beliefs, concepts, and tools.

Developing leadership knowledge comes from the awakening a leader has when they realize there is much more to learn and when the old ways of leading no longer work. You can see this progression in the above diagram. Leaders become aware of new thinking, and even though they are not sure what is ahead, they need to take a leap of faith that they will learn new principles and methods that will help them achieve more progress and success in the future. They are exposed to new concepts and tools, use

Developing Leadership Knowledge

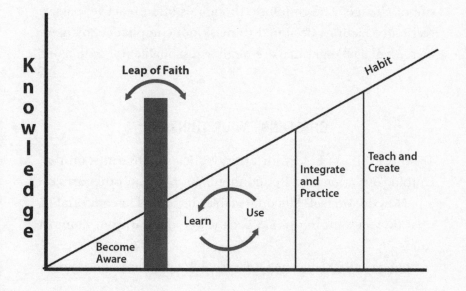

them over and over, and then they are able to teach and guide others. They often change their personalities and attitudes. They shift from arrogance and micromanaging to guiding and helping. They help other people develop to their fullest potential. An organization's fullest potential in action will help transform the enterprise. When leaders realize that their *primary role* is not to make money, but to lead people, adapt continually, and create an organization that will survive and innovate—and only when a natural leader is curious and wants to learn—can the journey to transformation commence. Transformation requires an open mind, never-ending questions, a deep commitment to change, and courage. The first question leaders must ask is, "Where do we begin—and why?"

Change (and change management) has become a popular, overused, and misunderstood word in organizations. Hundreds of organizations hear the mandate for change. It comes from Congress, the Pentagon, government agencies, the senior military, corporate executives, school superintendents, and others. Leaders and their organizations are compelled to respond to the mandate. They attempt to "talk the talk" and take action in pursuit of change. The response, though, is often reactive: passive resistance, actions designed to mask noncompliance, or mere incremental changes that are neither sustainable nor systematic.

CHALLENGE YOUR THINKING

Try this exercise: Fold your arms. Notice which arm is on top. Unfold your arms now. Refold them, but put your other arm on top. How do you feel? Uncomfortable? If you feel uncomfortable, what do you want to do? Go back to the old way, your comfort zone?

Change at first feels uncomfortable. It takes time and practice and a dedication to pivot, adjust, adapt, and do something different. Be patient with a disruption to the norm, discomfort, and change.

All improvement means change. We like improvement. But often if we suggest that something needs to change, we meet resistance. People often resist change because they have a fear of the unknown. Discard the word **change** in your vocabulary; replace it with the word **improve**. You will meet less resistance to making improvements and have much more success.

—

Unfortunately, few individuals understand the different kinds of change and the strategies and methods necessary to accomplish change. When you choose to survive, you make the decision to move forward. You must put action behind your words. You have learned several new ways of thinking about innovative leadership in the previous chapters. Now it is time to challenge your current thinking. How will you assess the thinking, decision making, culture, systems, processes, communication, and work flow of your organization?

Bring your team together and be clear about your purpose: to challenge the beliefs and assumptions about all of your processes, structures, practices, and rewards and incentives. Question everything! Let the team know that unless the organization is transformed for optimization, the organization will not succeed. Together the team needs to go to nirvana. No one can describe nirvana or how it feels, but you'll know it when you experience it.

But first, the team must begin its exploratory journey by questioning: What do we do? Why do we do it that way? What is the aim of that process? How could we eliminate it, or what are the opportunities to innovate? If there were a possibility that we could fail next month and close our doors, what could we do to save the company and survive?

THE THREE KEY COMPONENTS OF THE TRANSFORMATION PROCESS

There are three key factors any organization needs for transformation: an awakening, an intention to transform, and an openness to learn. First, an individual must be awakened to the discrepancy between his or her own thinking and the reality of the system's failure. Next, the individual must set their intention to face the issue and become committed to transformative change like never before.

STEP 1: AWAKENING

Transformation, which is necessary for any organization to survive, starts with the awakening of the individuals within an organization. This awakening begins with a challenge or a question (or a two-by-four upside the head!). It brings more questions—not answers. It is not a new way to do business; it is a new way to develop how to think, manage, and lead. It is the realization that, in spite of best efforts, the team or organization in question could do things better (improvement strategy) and differently (innovation strategy). There should never be negative repercussions to the individual because they did not recognize the need to transform sooner.

STEP 2: INTENTION

People within a system cannot see the system itself. If knowledge existed within the organization to solve a problem, then the problem wouldn't have occurred. Great leaders are those who ask for help. They do not chase the "flavor of the month" or the latest management fad; they go through a rigorous process to find coaches with profound knowledge.

Most managers do not have a theory of management they use to lead their organizations. What they do have is a tradition of unguided best efforts, handed down from supervisor to subordinate. In the absence of theory, there is only luck. I often encounter the accepted norm of "If things look OK, don't rock the boat, just make the numbers."

Without intention, both individual and organizational transformation are reduced to change. This discrepancy is comparable to the difference between memorization and learning, only more profound. Deeply motivated intention occurs after the awakening, creating a new mindset. The new view is not present yet—just the openness to *accept* a new view. It is possible that someone can have good intentions to transform and to do the work required to learn *without* the awakening, but in that case, the learning and transformation will be gradual. Once the awakening occurs, even if it occurs after the start of learning, the rate of transformation will increase exponentially, and previously "learned" lessons will gain greater significance.

STEP 3: LEARNING

Leaders must predict and anticipate. Prediction without information and knowledge is guessing. Knowledge is obtained through learning. Several authors (Deming, Senge, and Joiner) have noted that knowledge for transformation must come from the outside (i.e., external education and coaching.)

The "S-shaped learning curve" illustrates the need for transformation and new learning for the next level of growth. If the organization does not transform when it needs to, it will not survive.

Knowledge without action is the accumulation of trivia. Action is the application of new learning (the theory of knowledge). New learning occurs when the PDSA cycle is rigorously adopted, and multiple cycles bring new learning. Leadership requires action. Action, however, must be managed. This can be accomplished through the Plan-Do-Study-Act (PDSA) cycle, illustrated below:

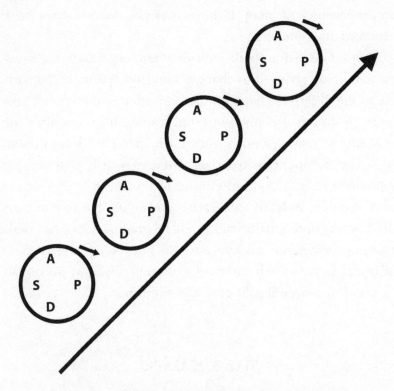

PDSA for Learning & Improving

An organization's use of multiple stages of the PDSA cycle offers continual learning. The more that people learn together, the greater their potential for a competitive edge. It is difficult to see the big picture when you are staring at a bunch of individual dots on a page. Connecting the dots (data) randomly can lead to a distorted picture, or even no logical picture at all. When you realize that you may not be looking at the right thing, it is important to ask for help. Learn the strategies for connecting the dots so that you can see the big picture or a different picture.

EXERCISE

Identify an example of three things that could affect your industry within the next five years.

1. Read industry newsletters or journals. What issues are they talking about?
2. What is happening globally that may impact your products or services?
3. What advances in technology or science may impact how your customers use your products or services?
4. What laws and regulations are being discussed that may impact your products or services?

THE FORMULA FOR EFFECTIVE CHANGE

Below is a change formula that helps identify the steps in the change process and the barriers that can prohibit rapid, effective change. Using this formula helps people overcome the resistance to change.

D x R x V x N x I = Effective Change
D = Dissatisfaction
R = Readiness
V = Vision
N = Next Steps
I = Integration

DISSATISFACTION

When an issue or problem exists within an organization, people become dissatisfied with the current situation. Some people are either in denial and live with the problem or are complacent and say, "That's the way it's always been." But natural leaders raise the level of dissatisfaction to create the movement for action and therefore the awareness about an issue. They see dissatisfaction as an opportunity to make things better or to solve a problem, or to find a new way to serve a customer.

READINESS

When a process needs to be improved, a task done, or a problem solved, sometimes one person can make a change that results in an improvement, but oftentimes it takes people working together. Those people may need to get ready for a change that has the potential to repair education or training, resources and tools, or coaching. Helping people prepare for change is critical. If this does not happen, people can experience a fear of failure and therefore resist a change. Identifying how to help people prepare for change and ensuring them that they will be supported and will not experience a loss will help a propel the change forward.

VISION

When there is a need for change, a natural leader will likely have a vision of what the situation will be when an improvement has been made. They can imagine the impact of a problem being solved, a process flowing smoothly without complexity, and a customer being satisfied. The natural leader then effectively communicates that vision to his/her peers to engage their cooperation in making it happen. The vision has to be stronger than the dissatisfaction. Otherwise people can tolerate the dissatisfaction they feel if the vision is not compelling enough for them to act.

NEXT STEPS

Small steps toward the vision can now be planned and implemented. The first steps may be awkward and uncomfortable, but the goal (the vision) will be powerful enough to drive the change

and overcome those fledgling first steps. The key is that you persevere with the purpose clear about the intent and commitment
to change for the better.

INTEGRATION

When the steps for change are implemented repeatedly and they
become more and more comfortable, the improvement happens.
All of the steps begin to work together, and feelings of accomplishment and success prevail.

Note: All change steps for improvement must be used. If any
one of them breaks down during the process, the desired change
can easily fail or be ineffective.

Here's a fun example almost everyone can relate to:

Johnny, age five, has an older brother, Sam, who is nine years
old. Sam and his friends love to ride their bikes to the park a
block away. Johnny wants to go, too, but he is not able to keep up
on his three-wheeler. He is tired of being left behind (dissatisfaction). He decides he is going to learn how to ride a bike, too.
When his dad comes home from work, Johnny asks, "Dad, can we
go get a bike for me, and will you help me learn to ride it?" That
Saturday, Johnny and his dad set off to buy his new bike so Johnny
can learn how to ride it (readiness), and then ride to the park
with the other kids (vision). Johnny begins to pedal as his dad
runs alongside the bike and holds the back of the seat to keep it
upright. The bike wobbles and jerks and Johnny fights to keep it
balanced. Steering, braking, balancing, and pedaling are all new
steps; nothing feels natural (next steps). But with a little practice,
Johnny is able to integrate smoothly all of the various actions:

steering, balancing, pedaling, and braking. Soon he is able to run out of the house, jump on his bike, and ride to the park with Sam and his friends (integration).

OBSTACLES TO CHANGE AND IMPROVEMENT

If change and improvement do not happen, you must ask yourself, why not?

Common reasons why change does not happen include:

1. The steps of the Change Formula have not been applied. Go back and go through the step that was overlooked or incomplete.
2. Individuals or a team get stuck in complaining and venting, or in complacency; they overfocus on the problem and never move to the options, alternatives, and solution phase.
3. People rush to a quick fix without really understanding the issue. They treat the symptom instead of the root cause of the problem, so the problem comes back, often over and over again.

Identifying and overcoming common pitfalls to change allows more improvements to materialize. When that happens, more people can become self-motivated to help make a difference.

EXERCISE

Identify an example of something you would like to improve, then answer the following questions to experience the change process.

1. What is the problem that needs to be fixed or the issue that needs to be improved? What is causing the dissatisfaction?

2. What is needed to prepare for making an improvement (training, resources)?

3. What will the improvement look like? What will make it better?

4. What first and second and third steps can be taken toward the improvement or solution? What feelings of discomfort or fear might be experienced?

5. What steps will you take to overcome awkwardness and fears to experience a better solution and improvement?

THE OLD WAY VS. THE BETTER WAY OF MANAGING

It's common for executives to spend much of their time answering questions to fix problems. But fixing problems is often reactive, and it's typically the case that the problems will pop up again, either in the same or in different places. Short-term thinking often leads to the question, "What problem are you trying to solve?" We have gotten used to it. Companies are founded on it. The large consulting firms ask it, then consultants retreat to their laptops to regurgitate another revised PowerPoint deck based on one they used last month or last year for another client. Their intentions and best efforts are commendable. They do want to help provide assistance (and make their quota for billable hours), but they don't have the systems and statistical knowledge required to help a company build out a sustainable future, and ultimately survive.

THE PRESIDENT

A progressive CEO in the golf industry asked Robert, one of his presidents, how he was developing his staff's leadership, team-building, and process improvements. In Robert's division, managers worked but they didn't work together. They met once a month, but never discussed the business. Instead they met and went on a field trip to visit a competitor's operation and have lunch. That was the "team." Robert asked me to help his team improve the business and their precarious financial challenges.

We created a different agenda, and the managers began to discuss the important business issues they faced, the severe competition and the declining industry, the direction they wanted to take the business, and the strategies they would need to move forward.

Robert had thirty years of experience using an old management style (listed below). There was a better way, but in his thirty-year career, he had never been introduced to it. In fact, most managers managed like Robert did—until now. I shared two management styles with Robert—the old way and a better way. He looked at the list of old ways and better ways. He recognized himself in the old way. He pointed to the better way and asked, "Can I do these instead?" His personal transformation was beginning. I nodded Yes.

Robert identified internally with the better way of managing. He had a choice, and it made him feel better. Almost immediately, he stopped using the old ways; he didn't like them, and they didn't feel good, but it was what he knew and how he had been managing for those thirty years—with a boss-subordinate mentality. Unfortunately, those old ways weren't how to lead and inspire people, move an organization forward, and have control of the business. His managers and staff were surprised by the quick shift their president made to abandon his old way and adopt the better way. The president's assistant and colleagues whispered, "What happened? What did you do to Robert? This is great, but will he change back?" I assured them that he is on a journey (as they all are) to improve their learning and leadership. People may take one step forward and two steps back when they are under stress and revert back to their "comfort zone." There will be rocky spots that may require the team to again look outside the organization for guidance, but the team must support one another throughout the entire journey.

Within weeks, the management team gave up their field trips.

Instead, we met, and I guided them to answer the questions on the Strategic Compass. They studied principles about systems and transformation and improving processes—all new concepts they had never heard before. The collaboration throughout the company blossomed as they began to learn and worked together. Information sharing and work flowed; together they made improvements that would link to greater customer experiences. Over the next few months, a healthier culture emerged, and teams began working more diligently on making improvements. The leadership team faced some huge financial challenges in a very competitive market and a rough economy. But they learned how to create a system and plan to innovate. This would transform the business. The president made a comment that is frequently heard among leaders with new knowledge: "I wish I would have learned how to lead people and transform my business earlier in my career. At least now I can share what I'm learning with my son who is in college—he's not learning these concepts there, either!" Adopting and applying new thinking and learning is invigorating.

So, what happened to this company? Did they survive? A new board president who was in an ugly internal battle fired the CEO, and a new one was hired. The new CEO lacked any leadership and transformation knowledge and joined the company with one objective that the board demanded: to cut costs. The president offered to present the Innovation Plan, but the new CEO wasn't interested. She believed that she would only keep her job by showing how proficient she was at cutting costs. It was her way or the highway. Unfortunately, as I've explained through many of these examples, "cutting costs exclusively" is a poor, but rather common, knee-jerk strategy for growth. There are hundreds of case studies of Fortune 1000 corporations who have drastically cut costs and either failed or are currently suffering a slow, painful demise.

However, leaders who guide a system use three significant interdependent strategies: improvement, innovation, and quality. Those organizations have a much greater probability for survival because they embrace new opportunities for success.

THE CONTROLLER

The Finance Controller in a client corporation deserved his title. Brian was very controlling. Every month I consulted with the management team and also had one-on-one meetings with the executives. It was rare for me to dread working with a client, but this particular manager was arrogant, condescending with his staff, and listened to no one except his friend, the company president. He was a coach's challenge, but also a great success story.

Over the months and years, he changed his thinking and behaviors. He shifted from being a cruel dictator to a compassionate leader. He began to interact and inspire his team differently. Eventually, he was promoted to the president's position when the president retired.

One day we were meeting in his office, and I noticed his eyes watering. Knowing that he wore contacts as I did, I assumed he had a piece of dust in his contact. A tear rolled down his cheek; then a tear rolled down his other cheek. I asked, "Are you OK?" He swallowed hard and said, "I was just thinking about how I used to treat people. I used to criticize, judge, and blame them. I never listened to their ideas. I thought I knew it all, and I made all the decisions, even about which copier to buy, and I never even used the copier! It was my way or the highway. No more."

Years later I was invited to be a keynote speaker at a conference. I asked if I could bring a co-speaker and the conference chair happily agreed. I invited the same president to share his story. We bantered and had fun sharing his leadership lessons.

He personally transformed and guided his company through some difficult years, but they not only survived—they did quite well.

The Old Way	A Better Way
Judges	Guides
Controls	Teaches
Criticizes, blames	Provide support/resources
Gives orders	Develops people
Demands results	Works together on process improvement
Dominates meetings	Encourages input, listens
One-way communication	Two-way communication
Avoids conflict	Deals with issues, with care
Creates fear, tension, stress	Reduces fear, builds trust
Always gives answers	Asks questions, creates healthy forum for discussion
"My way is the best way"	"We all need to contribute; no ONE has all the answers; many brains are better than one"
Uses power to get my way	Influence and engage with people
Stays in the office	Lead through interacting
Discounting behavior	Healthy listening & response
Lack of teamwork	Collaborate TOGETHER towards the aim
Boss is the customer	Internal and external customer focus
Opinions are given as facts	Use data & tools for decision making
Sub-optimizing system	Optimize the system
Lots of tampering with the system	Make decisions based on data
Functionally driven, departmental goals	Break down barriers
No discussion of the aim	Clear understanding of the aim
All projects hold the same importance	Prioritize & focus on key issues
No cross-functional communication	Cross-functional teams
High level of fear, anxiety, stress	Reduce fear, build trust

MANAGERS' AND TEAM WORKERS' PRINCIPLES TO PIVOT, DISRUPT, AND TRANSFORM

Organizational managers and teams often face an exorbitant volume of challenges. The overwhelming concern of "how do we reduce the complexity and achieve our aim?" is an ongoing one for the millions of people who go to work every day wanting to do a good job and make a difference.

Principles that effective managers and teams can adopt that will help them increase their productivity, quality, self-satisfaction, and meet customers' and citizens' expectations include:

1. **Create a compelling purpose and direction.** For
    example, in government, every employee begins his
    or her career with the following oath: *I, [name], do
    solemnly swear (or affirm) that I will support and defend the
    Constitution of the United States against all enemies, foreign
    and domestic; that I will bear true faith and allegiance to the
    same; that I take this obligation freely, without any mental
    reservation or purpose of evasion; and that I will well and
    faithfully discharge the duties of the office on which I am
    about to enter. So help me God.* Some never understand,
    and some forget that their true mission is to serve
    the people and carry out the will of Congress. A
    government buyer who spends forty hours a week
    purchasing toilet paper and cleaning supplies may
    forget that the supplies are to be used by troops
    risking their lives in war zones. Government service

is not a job. It is a lifelong dedication. Employee passion and motivation need to be directed to the mission, be it exploring space, protecting the citizens, or preserving the national forests. Agency and organizational goals must be interpreted within the overall purpose.

2. **Communicate the purpose so everyone understands how he or she fits into it and contributes to it.** Management is responsible for communicating the compelling purpose and goals hundreds of times daily and weekly. Yes, hundreds of times a day! If it feels like an excessive amount of communication, then leaders are probably just beginning to communicate well! They need to use multiple methods (email blasts, newsletters, town hall meetings, webinars, social media, videos, etc.). Workers or new hires need to understand how they fit in to accomplishing the aim of the organization, and that they are essential contributors to the aim. This is the job of management: to communicate effectively so everyone in the organization *understands* the link between him/her and their work and the customer they serve!

3. **Adopt beliefs that drive a focus for quality, continual improvement, innovation, and care.** Managers and any natural leaders believe in the value of improvement and positive change that helps customers. That belief set is then communicated with all managers and staff. Without a willingness to listen, learn from, and respond to input from all levels in the organization, management cannot create a change in beliefs. Employees will want to participate and provide ideas for improvement if they believe that management is serious and have their best interests in mind.

4. **Inspect what is necessary, but do not over-inspect
    and build in complexity**. Simplify, simplify, simplify!
    Bureaucratic processes become more complex over
    time. It is management's job to reduce complexity!
    Continually ask, what is the purpose?

5. **Continually improve every process so that quality,
    productivity, and trust improve, and waste and
    complexity are reduced**. Continually means on an
    ongoing basis.

6. **Create a robust, ongoing education and training
    (skills) system**. Training for skills is a cost of doing
    business; include resources for retraining the
    workforce as part of implementing improvements.
    Ensure that the workforce has the skills necessary for
    participating in the effort for continual improvement.
    Create opportunities for employees to meet and
    discuss issues, ideas, and possibilities for better
    outcomes.

7. **Develop a system for leadership in all employees.**
    The positional leaders need to adopt a mindset of
    humility, accountability, and courage with a passion
    for continual learning and listening to employees,
    customers, and partners. Drive out "leaders" who
    are controlling, narcissistic, egomaniacs, arrogant,
    or greedy. Natural leaders without titles or authority
    should be encouraged to contribute and use their
    influence.

8. **Reduce fear and build trust continually and intensely.**
    Become aware of the hundreds of fears in your
    organization and understand their impact on the
    people and organization as a whole. Ensure diversity
    (seniority, age, ethnic, cultural) is value-adding, not

value-diminishing. Managers who manage with fear and intimidation need coaching and guidance in how to improve their communication skills. Bullying is significantly increasing in schools and the workplace. Leaders must create a no-tolerance policy. Research shows that 40 percent of employees are bullied. Of that 40 percent, 80 percent are women bullying other women. Does that challenge your belief?

9. **Optimize the whole system.** Do not hold individuals accountable for the performance of the system. If the system does not deliver the results that are needed, change the system, don't blame the people. The people are responsible for contributing their part to help improve the system.

10. **Stop focusing on short-term results, numerical goals, and quotas.** Instead, focus on designing new systems that create better results—that improve the processes continually, removing the built-in flaws. Make decisions based on understanding long-term trends rather than making reactive decisions by looking at a single data point or comparing two single data points.

11. **Create a system of developing people through coaching conversations and informal, long-term mentoring.** Ensure that the organization's future leaders are committed to fostering a culture of continual improvement and innovation for survival.

12. **Encourage continual improvement for everyone.** Offer a robust system of education so all may understand systems and statistical thinking and how to use them. Create opportunities for nonstructured development as well, such as professional libraries, online learning, brown-bag lunches, and recorded videos of past discussions.

13.   **Create joy in learning and work.** Encourage employees
      to work together to transform the organization
      to new levels of innovation. Create opportunities
      for employees to have fun with coworkers to build
      relationships among staff and increase productivity.

AN URGENT TRUTH

DO YOU HAVE A CRISIS?

It was our first four-day off-site meeting with a global company in the chemical industry. The division manager and his management staff of fifty, mostly PhD scientists and engineers, were gathered to learn and avert an impending crisis that was looming over their industry. We were invited by Page, one of the directors who had influenced Bill, the division manager, to conduct the education session about the need to transform the company. The director expressed that only new learning and a new way to do business would prepare them to deal with the crisis over the next few years.

The first day began and rolled along with discussions, questions, and exercises. By 2:00 p.m. when we took the afternoon break, my colleague pulled Bill and Page aside and expressed some concerns. "They are not engaged; they are not taking this seriously." The division manager said, "Oh, I am sure they understand our dilemma and challenges." My colleague persisted, "No, they do not have a sense of urgency; they are complacent." Bill, because he did not feel any complacency, but knew that he could only move this organization if he had all his managers' help, was wary of this feedback. But he also knew that we had an outside perspective. Perhaps we could see what he could not see because he was in the system with these people every day. He pondered the possibility that we saw something new. During that ten-minute break, we helped him see another perspective. Then he had to help his team see what he saw. He had to communicate. He was their leader.

After the break Bill went to the front of the room and calmly asked the fifty people, "How many of you think we're in a crisis situation?" Five hands went up. At first Bill looked startled, but he went on to deliver a short ten-minute impromptu speech—and one of the most inspiring speeches I have ever heard.

"We live in nice homes, send our children to good schools, belong to the country club or the tennis club, and assume we have comfortable futures. But let me tell you how all of that could quickly change and why." He shared his concerns about the future, and he went into details about what the industry faced from global competition. "We are here to prepare for that challenge, as best we can. We need substantive change. That is why we are here. Over the next few days, we need to learn how to lead differently. We need to learn the new knowledge it will take to transform our organization for our people and our future."

The employees listened intently. They respected him. The commitment to new learning deepened immediately, and they shifted their focus. The remainder of the next three days took on a serious and deliberate mood. Up until this point, most of the fifty managers ran their departments as if their survival was a given. That day their leader shared a new perspective, and their mindset abruptly took on a deeper meaning and purpose. Survival was optional, and they had every intention to pivot and be survivors.

A FIRST STEP: AWARENESS

The first step in transforming requires the awareness of a faulty system (or one that is working today but won't be sometime in the future). The leaders must have the courage and be *self-motivated* to do something about it. Sometimes the leader needs to help his stakeholders recognize a crisis or an opportunity. Without his leadership, actions, and commitment to bring them together to learn how to transform, these fifty managers mentioned above would have continued on their current path. They would not have had the awareness or the ability to recognize the crisis facing the corporation.

This division manager had the insight to recognize the need for transformative change. In many cases, the leader may see problems, but often they don't see the impending crisis. And the leader may assume everyone else sees the problems, but often they don't. In this case, the management staff was not initially as motivated as the division manager because they did not realize the impact of not changing their thinking. Without clear directions and communication, the managers could be blindsided with too little time to recover. Either way, the leader then needs to help the entire organization work together for a better organization and future.

PERSONAL TRANSFORMATION

On another occasion, the ITT Division management executives gathered in the mountains above San Bernardino for an off-site retreat. It was the first time they had ever convened together to learn or plan as a "team." Just before lunch on the first day, the president said, "Marcia, it doesn't bother me that we don't know the answers to your questions because we are pretty smart, and we can figure out the answers. What bothers me is that I've been running this company for a long thirty years, and I've never thought of these questions." How could they know they had a lot to learn together?

They took on a new role as leaders for transformative change, creating systems to generate process improvements, new ways to question, plan, interact, and behave. More issues came to light that the managers had not previously recognized. Before when there were problems, they spent more time blaming and criticizing each other than focusing on how to improve the quality and serve their customers better. The team was beginning to form for the first time and to interact and listen to each other like they hadn't done before.

As we broke for lunch on day two, the president took me aside and asked, "Is there any way you can change your schedule and spend a third day with us?" The leadership team now shared an insatiable appetite for ideas that they had never been exposed to before. They were experiencing a robust focus on working together to understand their business and how to move it forward rather than point fingers at each other when they weren't getting the results they wanted. Their thinking was disrupted, and it was exactly what they needed.

Their personal transformations evolved over time. They built a momentum and sense of urgency to compete in an industry with commodity electronics products. Their will to survive and transform was now present and powerful. The president grasped every opportunity for his team to learn and work *together* rather than in their departments and silos.

My work with them over the next three years solidified their learning together (not without speed bumps) and the organization's growth. In a static industry, they became a cash cow for their division. While revenues continued to be stable and predictable, their profits increased times five. Personal leadership transformation led to the organization's transformation and survival.

WHAT GREAT LEADERS DO

Some individuals are natural born leaders. Other leaders are developed over time. In both cases, great leaders share some common characteristics. Great leaders think differently and ask tough questions. They tackle challenges. Great leaders display the characteristics of courage, authenticity, and humility. Great leaders don't walk away from tough situations or situations they don't like. They engage to understand, learn, and resolve issues. Great leaders speak up. Great leaders inspire. Great leaders never stop learning. Great leaders recognize, appreciate, and support. And great leaders are never complacent. They have the thinking and tools to keep a company not only in survival mode, but in a prosperous, optimized environment.

Great leaders inspire and develop their people and communicate with them to share a direction and a purpose. In his book *How Great Leaders Inspire Everyone to take Action*, Simon Sinek writes, "When a WHY is clear, those who share that belief will be drawn to it and maybe want to take part in bringing it to life. If that belief is amplified it can have the power to rally even more believers to raise their hands and declare, 'I want to help.' With a group of believers all rallying around a common purpose, cause, or belief, amazing things can happen. Inspiration only starts the process; you need something more to drive a movement."[9] Together, positional and natural leaders throughout an organization make a difference that alone they never could have accomplished. When a team is inspired, has a compelling purpose, and understands why they are working toward a common aim, their capabilities take on an exponential growth rate.

WILL YOU LEAD?

You completed the answers to the leadership self-assessment earlier in this book. How is your thinking evolving? Will you lead in a new, bold way? Harry Truman had a small sign on his desk that said, "The Buck Stops Here." A useful question for leaders is, "What is your essential role that you are accountable for and that you may not delegate?"

The leader must decide what the future of the organization is. It must be communicated to everyone so they understand how to contribute to it.

The leader creates the values from which the behaviors follow. There are articulated values, but the words and actions, behaviors and practices have to match and support the words. Many organizations say their values include collaboration, cooperation, and teamwork. However, they create "best practices" that include performance appraisals, employee of the month awards, incentives for achieving quotas or deliverables, and on and on. All of these create internal competition. They don't reflect the values that are articulated. But when I point this out to people, they are usually quite surprised. They had never thought about those inconsistencies before.

The leader has the strategic conversations and is deeply immersed in developing the strategic plan for the future. Once the aim and plan are communicated, the people work together to develop the methods to accomplish the plan, continually adapting it as they progress. The question transcends, "Are you getting the results you want?" The leader creates the environment for all employees to be *self-motivated* to learn, work, and improve together. When you ask the question, "What is the purpose of your business?" a leader does not answer: "To make money."

The leader focuses on a system that will generate products and service to WOW customers. Everyone in the organization understands that their job is to deliver what customers want, and to operate together. The focus is not solely to make money.

The leader thinks about the entire system. Many managers think, "We design it, make it, and try to sell it." Instead, leaders need to think about the entire system: design it, make it, prototype and test it, sell it, introduce it into the marketplace on a small scale, learn what the customers love, and go back to the design stage to integrate new, better ideas.

Leaders work ON the system. Employees work IN the system. All of the parts must work together and only the leader is accountable for whether the system can deliver the desired results. The leader (board, CEO) is accountable for the quality of the system. The customer defines quality.

THE GREAT LEADER'S ROLE IN THE SYSTEM

Great leaders discover problems and how to solve them and teach everyone in their organization how to do this, too. When continual improvement is one key strategy, progressing toward the strategy of innovation is next. When an organization has a culture of people contributing to improve, it will naturally follow that they will seek ideas to innovate and create new markets.

Leaders must be devoted to quality. Everyone must understand that principle. Cost cutting and laying off people to bolster a quarterly dividend or the stock price will send an unmistakable message throughout the organization that the only thing the employees are valued for is the contribution they make to the bottom line. A defining moment! This organization may not survive due to its leadership's thinking.

Executives and staff will succeed when leadership is at the foundation. Transformation will occur when there is a deep commitment to challenging current practices and generating new, continually improving processes focused on quality, leadership, trust, joy in learning, and pride in working together.

WHAT ABOUT YOU AND YOUR LEADERSHIP TEAM?

"Are you in or are you out?" This is one of the most profound and necessary questions you can pose. CEO Robert Rodin used it when he was leading Marshall Industries from $500 million to $2 billion in revenue over six years.

To be "in" or to be "out" is a choice. Every senior executive must make a deep personal admission that they don't know it all. They have to come to grips with their own thinking that their current reality is wrong. They don't know what they don't know. And they must have the courage to learn.

Reflect on it yourself. Are you on the journey of transformation? If not, your competitor or an innovator will be. Look at the current disruption in the taxi cab industry. Several new innovators like Lyft and Uber offer rides for about half the fare, tips included, and your bill arrives via e-mail. No more fumbling to pay as you're trying to get all of your belongings and get out of the cab.

Pose the question, "Are we going together in the same direction?" to your colleagues. You're all in the life raft, and you all need to paddle to the island. What if four of you are paddling in one direction and three in another? Do you want those three in your raft slowing you down and hindering your progress?

Pose the question, "Are you in or out?" to fellow leaders. Watch their actions, not their words. You don't want to see heads nodding yes now if you are only going to be sabotaged later. In Ron Heifetz's and Marty Linsky's book *Leadership on the Line: Staying Alive through the Dangers of Leading,* they provide valuable insights about creating an effective team. They write, "Some people simply cannot or will not go along. You have to choose between keeping them and making progress. Accepting casualties signals your commitment." Leaders have to make some tough decisions. Some people need to be let go when they do not want to go the same direction as the rest of the company. When those people leave the staff often breathes a sigh of relief and wonders, "What took so long?" When a leader acts to remove people who don't fit, the level of trust often increases.

INCLUDE YOUR NATURAL LEADERS

Natural leaders may or may not have a leadership title or position. Across the board, natural leaders are curious; they have a voracious appetite for learning and commit a significant part of their lives to searching, questioning, discovering, and experimenting. They fail often, but they consider failures and mistakes as part of life, another step on the journey to continually making life better. Courage is a common trait, but for a change catalyst, it's just part of how they think and act. Investing in your natural leaders' development is investing in your organization. Your natural leaders will be an asset with your staff. They can help model and implement change and encourage others to improve and innovate.

COMMON CONSIDERATIONS FOR NATURAL LEADERS INCLUDE:
- What changes can we make that will lead to significant improvement, innovation, and positive revolution?

- Not all changes require improvement, but all improvement requires change. How will we know that our changes result in improvements?
- Plan-Do-Study-Act (PDSA): This is the continual improvement change cycle first called the Plan Do Check Act (PDCA) cycle created by Dr. Walter Shewhart when he was at the AT&T Bell Labs in 1939. Dr. W. Edwards Deming used this continual change model as a four-step reiterative way to continually improve processes, products, and services.

Natural leaders stand out. They understand their purpose. They can clearly state and model their values. They are full of passion. Natural leaders face challenges and see them as opportunities.

EXERCISE

Make a list of your natural leaders.

1. What are the traits for natural leaders?
2. How can they help lead and influence more?

FROM TORY TO PIONEER

Butch, a young manufacturing engineer, worked at a global Michigan-based chemical company. He had a large, husky 6'4" build and a friendly, bold personality to match. His charisma was infectious, but he also knew that his passion to make continual improvements could be met with resistance from people who had been doing their work essentially the same way for twenty-plus years. One of the senior shop managers, Bob, was a thirty-year veteran and the union president. He had a reputation for being adversarial and set in his ways. Butch knew that if any transformation was going to happen, Bob was a key person to make it happen. Butch was self-motivated enough to influence Bob, and he took on the tough challenge. Manufacturing regularly had severe productivity challenges, yet effective changes for significant efficiencies were rarely implemented; the same issues faced and frustrated the managers and workforce for years. Sometimes, it was only by brute threats and force that the departments made their numbers.

Periodically at break time, Butch began to chat with Bob. They would talk about fishing and hunting and the latest football games. Weeks went by and the two men exchanged stories. One day, Bob was extremely irritated. Over coffee, Butch asked, "What's up?" Bob responded, "Oh, the same old crap; our production numbers are off, and management is riled up." "Maybe I can help. We can look at the process, collect some data, and see what's happening," Butch offered. Bob declined.

A week went by and once again Bob was frustrated and upset with the productivity results. Again Butch offered to help. Finally fed up with the same dreary results that he was getting over and over, Bob agreed to listen to how Butch could lend a hand. Together they looked at the process, collected and charted some data onto control charts, and saw the wild variation—ultimately, that the process was out of control. Butch explained to Bob what the new concepts meant and what the data showed. Based on that, Butch and Bob discussed some changes that could be made to improve the process. The changes were implemented, and the work and productivity began to improve. The data supported that progress was being made. At that point Bob asked Butch to teach him even more about looking at the production line and collecting the data.

Over the next few months, Butch and Bob not only worked on

a few processes, but Bob wanted all of the supervisors to learn how to look at their work and how to make improvements. The knowledge that Butch had about improving processes, focusing on quality, using statistical tools to collect data, and making better decisions was useful. Butch didn't have a big job, title, or position, but he did have strategic influence. He created a path to communicate, built a relationship, and eventually built trust with a positional leader who could make a difference. He set out to successfully help his company and catapult their competitive position in their industry.

THE BOHICA CURVE

The BOHICA Curve was first introduced to me by Lee Cheaney in Madison, Wisconsin and illustrates the interaction between Butch and Bob. BOHICA stands for Bend Over—Here It Comes Again. It details the mindsets of various people in the transformation process. Butch was a Pioneer, and (initially) Bob was a Tory. We'll go into the definitions of those terms in just a moment.

When new concepts are introduced within an organization and employees are encouraged to implement them, people react and respond to those in a variety of ways. The BOHICA shows and helps leaders understand the variation in thinking and behaviors by introducing the following categories:

Explorers: These people love new ideas and are risk takers; they have no fear and are natural leaders who experiment, learn, and push forward to discover what new progress they can make. They're a huge asset in any organization, though they are also like misguided missiles and can fire off without thinking things through. Making a plan is not their forte or what they excel at.

Pioneers: Like Explorers, this group is made up of natural leaders. They are eager to try new ideas and ways to improve or innovate. However, they have a special ability to not only persevere, but to plan ahead. They map out what they are going to do before they take action, and in this way are more thoughtful than the Explorers.

Settlers: The largest group in the organization. Their mindset to change is that while the ideas might sound ok, ultimately, they'll have to "wait and see" before they get on board.

Tories (From the British, a Tory is someone who opposes): The skeptics and cynics. This group doesn't like change, is not open to new ideas, and is resistant and usually vocal about their resistance. The hope is that there is not a Tory on the leadership team. Sometimes a Tory will verbally agree with the transformation efforts but will sabotage them or threaten his or her team to not support the efforts. Tories often like control over people and instill fear. Their resistance to change is often a deep fear of losing control.

Now what can you do with this information? It's common for leaders to invest their time and money training people across the organization. If it's a progressive organization, that can work. However, it's often more effective to first focus your investment time and dollars on educating, coaching, and guiding the Explorers and Pioneers. Help them achieve some initial quick successes. Share those "wins" with the rest of the organization. It is important for other employees and teams to see that not only can progress be made rapidly, but that mistakes can also be made and will be learning opportunities. People who make "mistakes" are viewed as leaders who experiment, learn, and move forward with that new learning. No one is punished for mistakes. Once the Settlers see the "wins," they move from their "settling" position to the Pioneer position: they adopt the natural leader mindset of, "We can make improvements, too."

Once the Settlers move, most of the organization has begun to transform. The journey for all begins and accelerates in a collaborative environment.

What happens to those Tories? At this point, there are a few options. If a Tory remains cynical, he may feel so uncomfortable in the new environment that he may choose to leave. Or, he may be asked to leave because the fit is bad. If, however, a Tory happens to be a co-owner, co-founder, or significant contributor to the success of the organization (example: a senior scientist or innovator), he may be moved to a single contributor position where he has limited influence on other team members.

Tories can also be capable of amazing transformation, as in the example with Butch and Bob. What happened there? Butch knew that he had to influence Bob and his approach that kept him frustrated and stuck with the production results. The only way to do that was to build a relationship and trust with Bob. Then Bob would be open to hearing Butch's ideas and learning from him.

Bohica Curves

Explorers: Grab the new ideas and run, often like misguided rockets

Pioneers: Like new ideas and plan how to implement them and do it

Settlers: "Wait and see," proceed if it is safe

Tories: Skeptics and cynics. But if they transform, they will be natural leaders

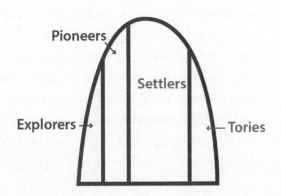

When this happened, and Bob wanted to learn more from Butch, Bob went from being a Tory to being a Pioneer. Bob transformed his thinking and his actions. Tories can transform and when they do, they make a significant difference because if they have a team of resistors, that team will transform, too.

What are you—a Tory or an Explorer? What are your team members?

GREAT LEADERS ANTICIPATE CHALLENGES TO TRANSFORMATION

Not all transformations will succeed. There are many things that can go wrong. Among them:

1. Leaders change. The efforts that began flounder and fail.
2. Tories in strategic roles can sabotage the process.
3. The leader can want transformation, but if the culture is resistant and he/she does not implement the "Are you in or out?" methodology in a timely manner, the transformation cannot succeed.
4. Some leaders want to transform but need to reach out to a guide for an outside perspective or another level of learning. Do they get help in a timely manner?
5. Some leaders espouse transformation as the "right thing to do." They've read the books or heard the words, but they have no intention of doing anything differently. They pay lip service but have no commitment or intention of transforming.
6. The motivations are "small thinking": what's in it for me versus what difference can we make with customers, the industry, or in the world?

Leaders combat barriers and accelerate transformation efforts. It is this type of commitment that an effective leader breathes every day, because they see no other option, and so much potential. Some leaders ask for help. Unfortunately, it's hard to discern when you first need outside guidance, and who has the knowledge you need to help you transform. Sadly, some people are hacks (they try hard but don't have the deep knowledge needed). Some coaches, consultants, and conference speakers can espouse improvement and innovation concepts. (I once attended a two-day innovation conference in Milwaukee; not one speaker spoke about or understood innovation; they all spoke about improvement strategies and did not understand the difference.) To guide leaders, it's essential to be able to teach systems thinking, system optimization, variation (though they might think Lean Six Sigma applies; it doesn't), motivation and learning, how all are connected, and how to communicate. How do you choose? Ask questions: ask about their knowledge, their approach, how they teach and guide, and how they have helped leaders achieve success and their challenges.

When executives communicate the aim of the organization and invest in their people by providing the environment and the education they need to learn, work, and improve together (system, process improvement, variation, etc.), their people will move them into the future. *Get out of the way of your people; they will take you to places you've never been before!*

ANALYTICAL VS. SYNTHETIC SYSTEMS THINKING

As leaders learn to transform their thinking, they shift from more analytical thinking to more synthetic, systems thinking. They move from focusing in on details (accounting, engineering, editing) to considering the strategies that need to be addressed to optimize the system. The decision making shifts from the details and the parts to the whole. Examining the details of a budget is analytic thinking. But identifying the measures of progress and success for a company is synthetic and necessary for the system.

The importance of the distinction between analytic and synthetic thinking is that as people move into positional leadership roles, they need to adapt their thinking for better decision making. If an accountant or an engineer becomes the CEO but maintains only analytic thinking (the thinking that may have been sufficient when working on projects), leading the organization with all of its interactive and interdependent parts will not be sufficient. Seeing and leading the organization as a whole system and guiding its direction requires the courage to ask a different and bold set of questions.

Leaders Shift from Analytic to Synthetic, Systems Thinking, from Analysis to Optimizing toward a Compelling Aim

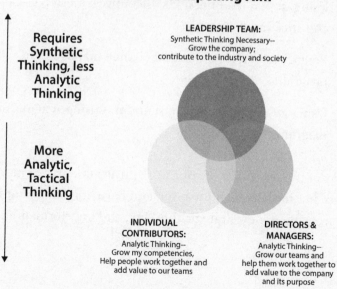

Requires Synthetic Thinking, less Analytic Thinking

More Analytic, Tactical Thinking

LEADERSHIP TEAM:
Synthetic Thinking Necessary—
Grow the company;
contribute to the industry and society

INDIVIDUAL CONTRIBUTORS:
Analytic Thinking—
Grow my competencies,
Help people work together and
add value to our teams

DIRECTORS & MANAGERS:
Analytic Thinking—
Grow our teams and
help them work together to
add value to the company
and its purpose

WHAT'S THE CATALYST FOR LEADERS WHO PIVOT, DISRUPT, AND TRANSFORM?

QUICK ASSESSMENT:

What is your organization doing? Check all that apply.

____ Benchmarking other companies

____ Holding individuals accountable for the outcomes of the system

____ Conducting performance appraisals

____ Setting arbitrary numerical goals

____ Using quotas, commissions, incentives, merit pay, carrot and stick methods

____ Practicing performance and change management programs

____ Using an organization chart and not using system diagrams

If any of these are part of your work environment, you may experience low morale, high turnover, and have huge opportunities for improvement, new strategic thinking, and transformation.

NEW STRATEGIC THINKING

Leaders believe there must be a better and bolder way. They are tired and frustrated of the status quo—the same old "fight for a larger piece of the competitive pie"—and they want to seize new opportunities and create a different future. They begin by discarding the archaic strategic planning process that they have endured throughout their career, and they start adopting a strategic thinking process that will challenge and accelerate their learning and working *together*.

Which one of these describes what happens in your organization:

_____ Leaders don't plan together; they're too busy running their business.

_____ Leaders go through a monotonous, well-intentioned process; there are few changes.

_____ Leaders eagerly engage in a robust, intense, provocative process to think, plan, and innovate.

General Eisenhower once said, while preparing for battle, that "plans are useless, but planning is indispensable." Planning is essential and reflects the strategic thinking it takes to create a plan that will be continually adaptable. If the plan is to be robust and responsive, that plan needs to be able to adapt to the challenges, opportunities, markets, and customer needs that arise. Robust planning provides the future direction for the organization.

The purpose of this section is to help leaders differentiate between creating a plan that goes stale—or one that creates improvements, innovation, a competitive edge, growth, collaboration, and success.

Traditional planning often engages people in limited discussions and few challenging questions. There are lots of pats on the back by well-meaning people as they meander down a path they've already been on year after year. They create "group think" (all heads nodding yes and no one asking tough questions) because no one is thinking differently. If the thinking is not different, you can't expect different outcomes from previous years.

Better, bold, new, and different results require new thinking and action:

1. Leadership does not delegate this role. An engaged leader is intimately involved in the strategic thinking and planning process (if not, how will they lead a new system?). This process is an essential part of their role.

2. Innovation in leadership knowledge. **The facilitator has systems and statistical knowledge** and facilitates the new learning and thinking necessary. The team learns a new way to innovate and transform their organization.

3. Openness to new learning TOGETHER. Together the team learns: how to question and challenge the status quo, how to reject the natural "we can't" excuses that stand in the way of innovation and transformation, and how to think with new knowledge and work TOGETHER through a bold, robust process of questioning what and why they aspire to a radical new level of success.

This focus is relevant for leadership teams in business, corporations, education, health care, nonprofits, and government/military.

TRADITIONAL VS. INNOVATIVE STRATEGIC THINKING AND PLANNING

Traditional planning is the linear thinking and language that fosters the creation of internal competition, fear, silos, and a toxic work environment full of blame, judgments, and criticism.

An alternative process is innovative strategic thinking and planning. This process is based on a theoretical foundation that includes systems thinking, understanding variation, developing knowledge, understanding the psychology of people, and the effective diffusion of communication.

TRADITIONAL PLANNING	INNOVATIVE STRATEGIC THINKING AND PLANNING
▪ Vision	▪ Aim/compelling purpose
▪ Mission	▪ Strategies based on a systems perspective
▪ Objectives	
▪ Goals	▪ Create quality, improvement and innovation as business strategies
▪ Targets	
▪ Tactics	▪ Values and behaviors develop the interdependent culture
▪ Numerical goals/specifications/metrics	▪ Customer needs defined and supported by data in context
▪ Budget by departments	▪ Experiential feedback
▪ Alignment	▪ Quality defined by the customer (markets)
▪ Quotas/incentives	
▪ Compliance/regulations	▪ Measures of progress and success (looking at data over time)
▪ Deliverables	
▪ Uses organizational chart, a hierarchical tool that does not include the customer	▪ Uses Strategic Compass
	▪ Uses System Diagram
▪ Uses Six Sigma tools, a target-driven tool that focuses on arbitrary numerical goals rather than understand what the system capability is	▪ Uses run/control/deployment flow charts
	▪ Plan Do Study Act model of continual improvement

CRITICAL DIFFERENCES

The essential differences between traditional and innovative strategic planning are:

TRADITIONAL	INNOVATIVE
▪ Linear/silo/department thinking	▪ Non-linear, interdependent thinking
▪ Old structure: vision, mission, goals, metrics	▪ New structure: aim/purpose, interdependent methods & results
▪ Groupthink and actions prevail	▪ Continual questioning of current beliefs, assumptions, practices, & results
▪ Acceptance of "we can't" due to rules/laws	
▪ Organizational charts are used to manage the organization	▪ Do the right thing; find/create the method
▪ Org charts don't include the customer	▪ Org charts are used only to understand who reports to whom
▪ Creates barriers and obstacles to work	▪ System diagrams are used that include the customer to optimize
▪ Communication is not cross-functional	▪ Facilitates reducing barriers/obstacles
▪ Use of arbitrary numerical goals and targets	▪ Communication flows throughout the systems and processes
▪ Language is fear based	▪ Data over time/in context are used
▪ Creates culture of fear	▪ Language allows possibilities/opportunities
▪ Individuals work hard, put in best efforts	▪ Focus is on reducing fear & building trust
▪ Expect different outcomes, but achieve the same or worse	▪ Work together collaboratively towards the aim
	▪ Outcomes are full of innovation, surprises, better than ever before imagined

THE CODE FOR BOLD CHANGE

We **must transform—not** merely change or improve—if we are to create a viable future. It will take leadership with profound knowledge and courage to have the stamina and commitment that transformation requires. Transformation is not easy, but it is critical to the health of our families and global society. Transformation is not for the other person to take on, but for every individual to take personal responsibility for to help create new futures, to ask questions, to take risks, and to make a difference.

Leaders need to prepare people for the journey. Leaders need to acknowledge the fears that improving processes will create. People fear losing their jobs, the unknown, making mistakes, speaking up. There may be strong resistance to change because the culture has already been established in the company. If some of the leadership team are also change-averse, surely the employees will feel uncomfortable, too. Employees may even observe their managers saying "yes" when reporting to *their* managers, but then doing nothing to support improvements. Why? Because the system was rooted in fear and driven by risk-aversion.

Improvement requires change, and change requires action. Across complex organizations, workers are challenged with obstacles preventing action for improvement. What gets in their way of making changes and improvements? How do people make the changes necessary? One significant barrier to improvement is employees not feeling like they have the opportunity to talk about changes. Making changes can feel very threatening to employees. However, if the leaders focus the mindset of the people on learning, working, and *improving* together, yes there will be change, but fear of the change will be diffused when people focus on *improving together.*

I've been invited to visit business owners, CEOs, university presidents, and executive teams to chat about the issues facing them and their organization. After an hour of interactive exploring about the problems they face, they may ask the significant question, "Where do we begin?" If they ask it, I know that they are committed to learning and transforming together. If they don't ask it, they're not ready to transform.

WHERE DO WE BEGIN?

We start with the three learning phases for transformation.

Phase One: A comprehensive system assessment.

Any leader who wants their organization to survive and innovate begins the journey with a coach who conducts this phase. This view into the organization summarizes the findings and recommendations through a new lens with new knowledge. The differentiator of this assessment compared to others is that the consultant asks the questions and makes the observations through a lens of profound knowledge described in Part Two. The lens strategy is based on a theoretical foundation of strategic systems thinking; analytical statistical thinking; psychology of people; motivation and learning; diffusion of communication; and leadership. In addition, barriers to quality, improvement, innovation, and trust are also identified. A summary report describes the findings and presents the initial steps and recommendations.

Phase Two: Creating an environment for an intensive, interactive learning/working session.

Based on the knowledge the leaders have, the next step for learning how to transform will be designed based on where the leaders' thinking and the cultural status is currently. Out of this experiential learning session, the leaders will have new ways to think, plan, and implement to accelerate their progress. For example, you can try to teach yourself to play the piano, but it is always better to have a teacher—someone to guide with knowledge and accelerate your learning (just like your transformation).

Phase Three: Putting the new thinking into action.

Asking: "What will we do different tomorrow morning? Will it make a difference for the long term? What is our plan based on our new thinking?" Learning and understanding systems management principles and beginning to apply them using many of the questions and models introduced in this book will help managers pivot, disrupt, and transform themselves and their organizations. If they adopt "excuse thinking" and delegate their leadership work to committees, nothing will transform.

In Robert Rodin's book *Free, Perfect and Now,* he writes:

"There are no shortcuts to systemic change…Fire, ready, aim! doesn't work. You have to plan, experiment, then study the result and plan again, working up a continual cycle of design, test, and improved redesign that engages the entire organization…Consensus isn't required; you're not running a democracy. However, you do need to get people coordinated to move in the same direction. You can't push them up the hill, whether you manage ten people or ten thousand. There are too many individual biases that will dilute your vision. Instead, you have to market your ideas one to one, patiently reaching out to potential change agents who can help you pull the rest of the company up the learning curve."[10]

FINAL WORDS

With fresh thinking, planning, and learning *together*, survival is possible. As leaders, we want to do more than just survive. We want our organizations to thrive. Like survival, thriving is a choice. It takes courage and lifelong commitment. But once a leader begins the journey, there is no going back. The learning and the experiences are powerful. Leaders see the need to pivot, create new industries or markets, disrupt the status quo, and transform. Great leaders have courage and knowledge that will guide them into the future.

Think Different. Act Different. *Be Different.*

GLOSSARY

AIM/PURPOSE

An end to be attained and a direction in which to move. It says what we are trying to accomplish together, what we want to be known for, and where we want to be in the future. It concerns a clarification of values the management holds for its stakeholders and the community at large. It is not defined in terms of activity or methods, but should relate to the foundation against which these should be checked.

COMMON CAUSES

Factors that are inside the system, inherent to the operation, and responsible for most of the variation.

COMPLEXITY

Obstacles and barriers to good quality and productivity. The root cause of the problems, unnecessary work and rework in processes which usually are found in inefficiencies, breakdowns and delays, mistakes and defects, variation.

CONTROL CHARTS

A graphic record of data which quantitatively describes a system's normal behavior and the variation in it. It depicts if the system is in or out of control, whether it is predictable or unpredictable. Management's job is to predict; they have to get the system into control.

CONTROL LIMITS

Limits that are derived from process data that describe the range of variability in the process.

CUSTOMER   The most important element of the process and
                       system. Someone or something receives the output
                       of a process. The process is designed to meet the
                       needs of this person/object.

DISRUPT   To uproot the normal way of thinking, acting, or
                       functioning in a business to produce something
                       more effective, whether in the marketplace or soci-
                       ety.

EMPOWER   To give permission to others (example: managers
                       give permission to employees to act); instead, great
                       leaders create the environment so employees are
                       self-motivated to use their power and contribute. (It
                       would be helpful if "empower" was not used in en-
                       vironments wanting to transform.)

FEEDBACK   Expectations of the customer. It directs the supplier
                       to learn about the disparity between the "Voice of
                       the Customer" and the "Voice of the Process."

FLOW CHARTS   The steps showing the sequence and flow of the
                       work, and the input and output and the decision
                       points. They show the process as it works, in its sim-
                       plicity or with its complexity.

PDSA   The Shewhart Cycle of Continual Improvement,
                       often noted as the Deming Cycle. A powerful mod-
                       el to Plan-Do-Study-Act.

PIVOT   To shift a mindset or business strategy to reposition
                       an organization for success.

PROCESS   Step-by-step flow of the work. It transforms inputs
                       into outputs.

PROFOUND KNOWLEDGE Rare, uncommon, and interdependent bodies of
                       information used for transformation.

QUALITY

A judgment made by a consumer or user of a product or service. It is determined by top management and cannot be delegated.

SPECIAL CAUSES

Assignable, atypical events from outside the system, which affect variation inside the system.

SUPPLIER

Someone or something that helps create a process and its output for the customer.

SYSTEM

A network of interdependent parts that work together to accomplish the aim of the system and produce the outputs for the organization.

TRANSFORM

To create and change a whole new mindset, form, function, or structure.

VARIATION

Changes, deviations, and differences that can be found in all products, services, systems, and processes over time. Everything has variation. It can be managed and reduced, but never eliminated.

VOICE OF THE CUSTOMER (VOC)

Communicates the desires, wants, and needs of your customers.

VOICE OF THE PROCESS (VOP)

The output or results that the system or processes are able to deliver.

BIBLIOGRAPHY

Ackoff, Russell. *Idealized Design*. Wharton School Publishing, 2006.

Adler, Alfred. *Understanding Human Nature*. Hazelden, Center City, MN: 1998.

Arbinger Institute. *Leadership and Self Deception. Second Edition*. Berrett-Koehler Publishers, 2017.

Argyris, Chris. *Overcoming Organizational Defenses*. Allyn and Bacon, Boston: 1990.

Baker, Edward. *The Symphony of the System of Profound Knowledge*. iUniverse, 2017.

Berger, Jonah. *Contagious: Why Things Catch On*. Simon & Schuster, 2016.

Blanchard, Ken and Renee Broadwell. *Servant Leadership in Action*. Berrett-Koehler, 2018.

Block, Peter. *Community: the Structure of Belonging*. Berrett-Koehler, 2009.

Burrus, Daniel. *The Anticipatory Organization*. Greenleaf Books, 2018.

Cheaney, Lee. Contributed the first introduction to the BOHICA curve. 1992.

Coens, Tom, and Mary Jenkins. *Abolishing Performance Appraisals: Why They Backfire and What to Do Instead*. Berrett-Koehler Publishers, 2002.

Covey, Stephen R., *The Seven Habits of Highly Effective People*. Simon and Schuster, New York: 1989.

Dalio, Ray. *Principles*. Simon & Schuster, 2017

De Bono, E., *Six Thinking Hats*, Little, Brown, and Co., 1999.

Delavigne, Kenneth and Daniel Robertson. *Deming's Profound Changes: When Will the Sleeping Giant Awaken?* Prentice Hall, 1994.

Deming, W. E., *The New Economics*. MIT Press, Cambridge: 1993.

Deming, W. E., *Out of the Crisis*. MIT Press, Cambridge: 1986.

DePree, Max. *Leadership Jazz: The Essential Elements of A Great Leader*. Crown Business, 2008.

Duhigg, Charles. *The Power of Habit: Why We Do What We Do in Life and Business*. Random House, 2014.

Fried, Jason, and David Heinemeier Hansson. *Rework*. Crown Business, 2010.

Gharajedaghi, Jamshid. *Systems Thinking*. Butterworth – Heinemann, Boston: 1999.

Gill, Libby. *The Hope-Driven Leader: Harness the Power of Positivity at Work*. Diversion Books, 2018.

Gluckman, Perry, and Diana Reynolds Roome. *Everyday Heroes of the Quality Movement: from Taylor to Deming, the Journey to Higher Productivity*. Dorset House Pub., 1993.

Goldratt, Eliyahu M., and Jeff Cox. *The Goal: Beating the Competition.* Creative Output, 1986.

Heath, Chip and Dan Heath. *Made to Stick: Why Some Ideas Survive and Others Die.* Random House, 2007.

Heifetz, Ronald A. and Linsky, Marty. *Leadership on the Line.* Harvard Business School Press, Boston: 2002.

Horowitz, Ben. *The Hard Things about Hard Things.* Harper Collins Publishers, 2014.

Jeffers, Susan J. *Feel the Fear– and Do It Anyway.* Ballantine Books, 2007.

Joiner, Brian L. *Fourth Generation Management.* McGraw Hill, New York: 1994.

Johnson, H. Thomas and Anders Broms. *Profit Beyond Measure.* Free Press, 2008.

Kaye, Beverly and Sharon Jordan-Evan. *Love 'Em or Lose 'Em: Getting Good People to Stay,* 2014.

Keirsey, David and Bates, Marilyn. *Please Understand Me.* Prometheus Nemesis, Del Mar, CA: 1984.

Kohn, Alfie. *Punished by Rewards.* Houghton Mifflin Harcourt Publishing, 1999.

Kouzes, James and Barry Posner. *The Leadership Challenge.* Jossey-Bass, 2012.

Langley, Gerald, et al. *The Improvement Guide.* Jossey-Bass, 2009.

Liker, Jeffrey K. *The Toyota Way.* McGraw-Hill, 2004.

Miller, Lawrence M. *Barbarians to Bureaucrats.* Potter, New York: 1989.

NBC and Clare Crawford-Mason. *If Japan Can, Why Can't We?* (documentary), 1980.

Nonaka, Ikujiro. *The Knowledge-Creating Company.* Harvard Business Review Press, 2008.

Orsini, Joyce. Editor. *The Essential Deming.* McGraw-Hill, *2013.*

Petty, Priscilla. *The Deming of America (video).*

Pfeffer, Jeffrey. *Leadership BS.* Harper Collins, 2015.

Pink, Daniel H. *Drive: The Surprising Truth About What Motivates Us.* Riverhead Books, 2011.

Provost, Lloyd and Sandra Murray. *The Health Care Data Guide.* Jossey-Bass, 2011.

Rodin, Robert. *Free, Perfect, and Now.* Simon and Schuster, New York: 1999.

Rodin, Robert and Backaitis, Nida. *Beyond The Sounds Of Silence* (unpublished monograph): 1995.

Rogers, Everett. *Diffusion of Innovations.* Free Press. 2003.

Rother, Mike. *Toyota Kata: Managing People for Continuous Improvement, Adaptiveness, and Superior Results.* McGraw-Hill, 2010.

Ruiz, Don Miguel. *The Four Agreements.* Amber-Allen Publishing, San Rafael, CA: 1997.

Schein, Edgar. *Process Consultation Revisited: Building the Helping Relationship.* Addison-Wesley, 1999.

Scholtes, Peter R. *The Leader's Handbook.* McGraw Hill, New York: 1998.

Senge, Peter M. *The Fifth Discipline, revised.* Currency Doubleday, New York: 2006

Shewhart, Walter A., and W. Edwards Deming. *Statistical Method from the Viewpoint of Quality Control.* Dover, 1986.

Sinek, Simon. *Start with Why: How Great Leaders Inspire Everyone to Take Action.* Portfolio/Penguin, 2013.

Thomas, Kenneth. *Intrinsic Motivation at Work.* Berrett-Koehler Publishers, 2000.

Wheeler, Donald J. *Understanding Variation: The Key to Managing Chaos.* SPC Press, 2000.

Yoshida, Kosaku. *The Joy of Work* (published in Japan in Japanese) *2007.*

ENDNOTES

1. *Abolishing Performance Appraisals: Why They Backfire and What to Do Instead*, by Tom Coens and Mary Jenkins, Berrett-Koehler Publishers, 2002, p. 19.
2. *Rework*, by Jason Fried and David Heinemeier Hansson, Crown Business, 2010, p. 135.
3. *Anticipatory Organization*, by Daniel Burrus, Greenleaf Book Group, 2017, pp. 128–129.
4. *Understanding Variation: the Key to Managing Chaos*, by Donald J. Wheeler, SPC Press, 2000, p. 107.
5. *Toyota Kata: Managing People for Continuous Improvement, Adaptiveness, and Superior Results*, by Mike Rother, McGraw-Hill, 2010, p. 166.
6. *The Knowledge-Creating Company: How Japanese Companies Create the Dynamics of Innovation*, by Ikujiro Nonaka and Hirotaka Takeuchi, Oxford University Press, 1995, p. 157.
7. *Intrinsic Motivation at Work: Building Energy & Commitment*, by Kenneth W. Thomas, Berrett-Koehler, 2008, p. 65.
8. *Drive: The Surprising Truth About What Motivates Us*, by Daniel H. Pink, Riverhead Books, 2011, p. 81.
9. *Start with Why: How Great Leaders Inspire Everyone to Take Action*, by Simon Sinek, Portfolio/Penguin, 2013, p. 136.
10. *Free, Perfect, and Now: Connecting to the Three Insatiable Customer Demands*, by Robert Rodin and Curtis Hartman, Simon & Schuster, 1999, p. 69.

APPENDIX

---

14 POINTS FOR MANAGERS

1. Create constancy of purpose toward improvement of product and service, with the aim to become competitive and to stay in business, and to provide jobs.
2. Adopt a new philosophy. Take on leadership for change.
3. Cease *dependence* on inspection to achieve quality.
4. End the practice of awarding business solely on the basis of price. Move toward a single supplier and build a relationship.
5. Improve constantly and forever the system of production and service, to improve quality and productivity, and thus constantly decreasing costs.
6. Institute training on the job to make better use of all employees.
7. Institute leadership. The aim of leadership should be to help people and machines and gadgets to do a better job.
8. Drive out fear, so everyone may work effectively for the company.
9. Break down barriers between departments. Work together in teams to foresee problems.
10. Eliminate slogans, exhortations, and targets for the workforce that ask for new levels of productivity without providing methods.

11. Eliminate quotas, MBOs, management by numbers, numerical goals. Substitute leadership.

13. Remove barriers that rob people of his/her right to pride in their work.

14. Institute a vigorous program of education and self-improvement.

SEVEN DEADLY DISEASES

- Lack of constancy of purpose (lack of direction or aim)
- Emphasis on short-term profits (Focus should be on the processes and improving them; if the systems and processes flow well, the results will be good.)
- Evaluation of performance, merit rating, or annual review (Focus on fixing systems, not individuals—it's a waste of time: judging, ranking, and rating.)
- Mobility of management: job-hopping
- Running a company on visible figures alone—the bottom line/$$$ (see #2)
- Excessive medical costs
- Excessive costs of liability

from *Out of the Crisis* by W. Edwards Deming, MIT Press, 1986.

ACKNOWLEDGMENTS

Once upon a time...I thought I'd like to begin to write a book with those few words. What would follow I wasn't quite sure. And then there would be The End.

What I've learned is that it takes a lifetime of learning and a community of family, friends, colleagues, students, challengers who provoke new thinking, and clients to create a book. Thank you. People, situations, travels, and lessons come and go. Some stick. Others are forgotten. People float into our lives for a minute or a month, share a powerful message, and then as seamlessly, they pass through on their journey never really knowing their impact.

The innumerable and mesmerizing encounters I have been so fortunate to experience in my life have led to the emergence of Pivot, Disrupt, Transform. It is from those meetings, some by chance and others enduring for decades, that I am so honored to say Thank You. So many people have helped me learn and make a difference. Those I am most grateful to are those across the decades and the world who created environments for me to learn, participate, lead, respectfully question, share, and contribute.

Thank you to those who encouraged and supported me through the writing and publishing process. Many thanks to the reviewers who, over the years of creation of this book, gave me feedback and asked me great questions. This book is solely written based on my observations, experiences, client engagements, deep conversations with colleagues, reading, and research for the past 25-plus years.

Special thanks to some of the busiest people I know who took the time to read my manuscript, believed in my messages, and endorsed my book. Thank you for stepping up! It takes leaders with courage!

Over a breakfast discussion, Stanford professor and author John Krumholtz and I chatted about a variety of topics including my half-written manuscript. His encouraging, profound comment inspired me, "Marcia, you've got to finish your book! No one else is talking about these messages, and you know how to apply them." I returned to the manuscript until it became a book.

I am deeply grateful to my book agent, Linda Langton; contract manager extraordinaire Jennifer Urum; the publishing team at Diversion Books; my developmental editors Leslie Stephen, William Croyle, and Kelly Maheu; my assistants, Joe Chedid, Shuyo Chang, Vanessa Riascos, Robert Frink, and Stephen Frink.

My communities that have evolved were especially sparked by one man: Dr. Perry Gluckman who introduced me to Dr. W.E. Deming and his philosophy of leadership. Bill Cooper encouraged me to "start a Deming study group" and the Bay Area Deming User Group (BADUG) and later the In2In Thinking Forum emerged with thousands of dedicated global participants.

Expanding the opportunities to make a difference, I speak to, contribute, and participate with other Rotarians; the Deming Institute; Santa Clara University and San Jose State University alumni and communities; and JDRF (in the search for the cure for T1Diabetes).

As I began this book, I'll wrap up this book. Special dedication goes to my family, my mentors, and my communities. May we all continue our learning journey, develop our natural leadership and courage, help others, and transform.

Thank you to those listed here (and many others are in my book) for your contribution:

Dan Burrus

Renee Broadwell

Mougahed Darwish

Brian Bates

Brian Henry

Art Darin

Harry Artinian

Jeevan Sivasubramaniam

Babette Shelton

Nida Backaitis

Sheila Sheinberg

Sheila Jordan-Evans

Leah Simon

Donna Friel

Sue Calhoun

Marian Hirsch

Ian Bradbury

Dan Robertson

Dick Steele

Joe Pinto

Joe Chedid

Stephen Frink

Robert Frink

Shuyo Chang

Vanessa Riascos

Kelly Maheu

Colleen Griffith-Regal

Phil Monroe

Austin Kim

Greg Conlon

Frank Kudo

Craig Siiro

Priscilla Petty

Eric Sandberg

Anchal Tiwari

Harry Artinian

Barry Cioffi

Brian Bates

Joe Onstott

Sandy Hart

Daniel Lebus

Debra Lewis

Taylor Gray

Peter Krasney

Mike Propkopeak

Joyce Musil Condon

Pamela Evans

Dr. Francisco Jimenez

Frederique Fechner

Christine Ascher

Kenji Furushiro

Libby Gill

Dr. Jerry Glass

Scott Graham

Bill Howell

John Howman

Mary Jenkins

Jim Leale

Cecily Joseph

Marty Kandes

Ken Kuang

Dr. Malek

Dr. Harmeet Sachdev

Dr. Nancy Mann

Richard Narramore

Kathy McAfee

Rick Gilbert

Kristen Franzen

Don Petersen

Brian Olmsted

Peter Stonefield

Jeffrey Pfeffer

Raymond Jung

Peter Redford

Rod Diridon

Mike Tveite

Bruce Winkler

Tom Bondi

Jennifer Urum

Karina Mikhli

Tatiana Lascu

Marshall Goldsmith

Neuwirth & Associates

Larry Smith

INDEX

ABOUT THE AUTHOR

MARCIA DASZKO has led her strategic consulting firm for more than 25 years. As Catalysts for Strategic Change, Innovation, & Transformation, she works with executive teams across all sectors to create bold, different, innovative leadership thinking, business models, strategies, systems, and new markets. She facilitates the dialogue and tough questions to accelerate healthy and exponential growth, profitability, and innovation. As a keynote conference speaker and graduate management professor, she is a dynamic provocateur and contrarian to the management fads and "best practices" that create internal competition and toxic work environments. Clients range from Fortune 500 corporations such as Apple, Boeing, Dow Chemical, ITT, Pepsi, and Varian Medical to global nonprofits, health care, education, and the U.S. Navy.

As a student of Dr. W. Edwards Deming and Dr. Perry Gluckman, she has devoted her career to spreading the leadership principles of her mentors and guiding organizations to apply them. She co-founded the Bay Area Deming User Group (BADUG) and was a co-founding board member of the In2In Thinking network, www.in2in.org. She is a board member and advisor on several education and nonprofit boards. She's also an avid supporter for the JDRF research to find a cure for Type 1 diabetes. She has been nominated to receive the International Deming Medal quality award.

Marcia lives in the heart of Silicon Valley, in Northern California.

Contact information:
www.mdaszko.com
www.linkedin.com/in/marciadaszko/
md@mdaszko.com